FLYING WITH GOD
Putting on a Happy Face

A Flight Attendant Memoir

Bettina "Sparkles" Obernuefemann

Harmony Hills Press

FLYING WITH GOD
Putting On A Happy Face

By

Bettina "Sparkles" Obernuefemann

Original Cover Art by Sparkles

Second Edition
Copyright © 2006

Sparkles will contribute 20% of net profit of sales revenue of this book to non profits committed to healing child abuse and supporting unwed mothers.

Printed in the United States of America
ISBN 0-9768782-8-3

DEDICATION

Michael, dear husband and friend so true,
I dedicate this book to you!

Freedom was your gift to me,
To find my true self and learn to be!

ACKNOWLEDGMENTS

I thank God for showing me the way Home.

I thank God for helping me find my Inner Child, my Inner Spirit.

I thank God for my parents for giving me birth and being my major teachers.

I thank God for my brother and his family.

I thank God for my Obernuefemann in-law family I met in 1990 and who accepted me unconditionally.

I thank God for America, still the land of great opportunities.

I thank God for my airline family.

I thank God for my family of choice and all my friends who believed in me more than I did in myself, especially my book supporters: Debi Miller, Suzanne Bruder, Mary Wilson, Mary Ann Patterson, Carol Risher, Joy Young, Peggy Jenny and Dr. Mark Weiss.

I thank God for Stella Steele's invaluable input and contributions. She had the gift to pick my brain, enter my heart and soul, help me express the real me and make the story flow.

I thank God for June Santonastasi for her work presenting my photos and Ronna Zinn for the final preparation to publish my work.

GOD IS DOING THE WRITING

To write, I have the desire,
God, please light my fire.
Inspire me every day,
Sparkle and lead the way.

Writing is a sure tool,
To add fire to the fuel.
It is a way to share,
To show that I really care.

It helps my scars to heal,
To let go of the pain I feel.
Being all One, not apart,
God's writing through my heart.

Bettina "Sparkles" Obernuefemann
7-15-2000

FLYING WITH GOD
Putting On A Happy Face

INTRODUCTION

As a veteran flight attendant, I chose the title *Flying with God* for this book and used the metaphor to describe my search for a better, more meaningful life— in other words, my spiritual journey. Are we not moving or flying through space, dependent on a Higher Source that we don't understand? Comparing life on earth to an airplane ride gave me a clearer view of our commonalities, our connectedness— our Oneness with our Higher Power or God or whatever name people give It. Once I recognized that we're all together in this thing called Life, I've come to understand how necessary it is that we help and love one another—just as Jesus taught us. And part of my realization is that we're not only all flying with the same one God, but also we're all flying with Him whether we are aware of it or not. But wait…I'm really getting way ahead of myself.

Please know, I haven't always been this introspective. It was not until 1985, after I turned 45, that I became a serious seeker and slowly began healing war and child abuse traumas, a recovery process I now focus on daily. Back then I was lucky to be living in the United States where the self help movement was well established. (Unfortunately, this phenomenon was postponed in my home country, Germany, by the succession of wars.) As it evolved over the years, it combined the investigation of child abuse, the fellowship of Alcoholics Anonymous and other 12-step programs, family systems theory, as well as the study of Post Traumatic Stress Disorder among the returning Viet Nam Vets. Driven to improve the human condition, many excellent writers intermingled ancient wisdom with consciousness raising, such as my heroes Wayne Dyer and Louise Hay. Even though the mental health and spiritual movements are still expanding rapidly, there are too many people who are not yet willing to take the first step.

This is especially true in my birth country of Germany, where very few survivors of WWII see the need to address their 60 year old pain or even know that treatment is available. But healing is so important—not only for survivors, but for their children—the cycle of fear must be broken! According to a special December 2003 issue of the German magazine, *Der Spiegel,* only 10% of the German psychologists and psychiatrists even consider any connection between anxiety, anger, depression or other mental disorders and the peoples' sufferings before and during WWII. These children, born between 1930 and 1945, (like myself) buried traumas under the ruins and focused only on rebuilding their lives and their country. Most of them wear a mask of courage, concealing their feelings of personal worthlessness and collective guilt, ignoring their pain without ever grieving their losses.

I feel a close bond with my fellow countrymen and all victims of war, civilian or military. In similar fashion, my heart goes out to all abused children who also might be keeping their secrets deep inside and are barely making it through life with only a façade of strength. Their story is my story, and my story is theirs. I, too, wore a mask while fear festered inside of me. Ironically, wearing my stewardess smile was a perfect cover for presenting my false self and hiding my real self and that is why I chose the subtitle of "Putting on a Happy Face."

In 1996, I sensed a strong inner nudging to share my story. That was much easier said than done, but I put on my recall cap and began to type and type and type some more and write and write some more. Digging, recalling and writing about my past added so much to my personal growth that I consider it my ultimate journal. It was truly an intensive time of learning—a time when "I put on my own oxygen mask before assisting others."

Often, I lost faith along the way and prayed for help and strength to continue writing, even living. And Help came. One morning in the summer of 2000, while I was meditating, an Inner Voice came through loud and clear.

"Once upon a time, as WWII's bombs fell from the sky above Germany's Ruhr district, a little girl was born. Her mother named her Bettina, "little Elizabeth." Bettina chose to be born during this dark period in human history so she could tell the world about the insanity of war.

Deep inside this little girl was a tiny spark that knew all about the Oneness and Love of God. Her purpose was to remind people of the way back to peace. But, as most humans do after they're born, she promptly forgot why she was here. Her childhood was filled with unbearable hurts, all of which she stuffed inside the bunker of her mind. Then, when she was fifty, she rediscovered her Inner Child, and all those suppressed memories surfaced. At that point, she had no choice but to admit to herself that, though she may have been smiling on the outside, all along she had been desperately crying on the inside.

It was then that she recalled her important mission. Guided by God, she began to write about the ups and downs of her turbulent private life and her long flying career. Because she was able to face and release her buried fears, Bettina's story has a happy ending. Yes, the more she was able to honor the spirit of her Inner Child, the more she was able to proclaim that *Flying with God* is the only way to fly!"

This message inspired me to keep on writing and by March of 2002, I had finished a rough manuscript. I realized then that my work needed help to make it flow. At the perfect time God sent me a wonderful free lance editor. Together we worked hard to show what life was like for the old Bettina in the "mask-wearing" survival mode. And, I am anxious to start my next book to show how I transformed my life by reclaiming my Inner Child or My Inner Spirit.

But, first things first. This book is about the *un*transformed me. In Part I, I explain my chaotic upbringing set against the terrifying backdrop of Germany during WWII. I tell of the travails I suffered while being raised by my domineering mother and passive father. The saga continues with my family's journey to the 'New World' and our many moves across Canada and the United States. I share how my dysfunctional upbringing always made me feel like an outsider and how "looking for love in all the wrong places" got me into big trouble.

In Part II, I take a nostalgic trip back to my early years of flying as I recount some interesting first hand, behind-the-scenes experiences. I also answer many of the questions that curious travelers have asked me over the years.

How long have you been flying?
Do you like your job?
Do you fly this route all the time?
Do you ever get scared?
Have you ever had famous people on board?

Dear readers, you may wonder why this lady is so willing to shatter her smiling flight attendant image by revealing her personal history and airing her family's dirty laundry. The answer is simple— during the last twenty years, I've developed a passion for inner healing and a desire to share that even the most hopeless situations can be overcome. To those of you who can relate to any part of my story but find yourselves stuck in a particular fear or pain, I'd like to say there is a way out—peace is at hand!

July 31, 2003, I retired after 38 years of flying. At that point, I had worked on my manuscript for seven years and had fine tuned it another year for publication. My editor suggested more tweaking, but I am willing to take a risk and present my story to you, as is.

Ladies and gentlemen, thank you for giving me the opportunity to serve you in the air and giving me the honor to continue to serve you with this memoir. And now, as any good flight attendant would, I invite you to sit back, relax and enjoy your flight through the pages of this book.

PART I

LIFE BEHIND THE SMILE

Chapter 1

Born Into WWII

I entered this world on October 24, 1940, in *Mülheim-Ruhr, Germany*. Ironically, my life began one year after the start of WWII, which caused millions on earth to lose theirs.

Why would anyone choose to come into this world in Germany at a time when most of its citizens had lost the will to live? Many were imploring "We have no work! We have no food! How can God allow all this horror?"

But my determined stork ignored the signs of the times, delivering me as he dodged the bombs falling all around him. My mother often talked about that night and how the sirens that signaled approaching bombers were screaming over City Hospital where she was in labor. She said, "When the danger was over and the sirens became quiet, my little girl cried her first cry!" Such was my welcome to the world! What baby would need a slap on the butt under these appalling conditions?

Times were really rough for *meine Mutter,* my mother. She was born in 1922, after Germany's defeat in WWI. The devastating loss left the country's citizens with a feeling of utter hopelessness, and they spent the next decade or so determined to pick themselves up. In their despair, they soon allowed themselves to become mesmerized by the unrealistic promises of the charismatic Adolf Hitler. In his countless speeches, he vowed to create a superior nation and increase Germany's territory. Many believed his fiery propaganda, only to discover later that they had been completely misled.

The first husband of my maternal *Oma,* Grandmother Maria, had died of pneumonia while returning home near the end of WWI. So she was left to fend for herself and her daughter, Lisbeth, during the hard post-war times. This half sister, fifteen years older than my mother, was the hero, talented in sewing and other crafts, and was of great help with all the household chores, including taking care of my mother, who had been born of Oma's second marriage.

Without actually espousing his politics, my mother transferred Hitler's rhetoric about a better Germany into her own dream for a better life. In her teens, my mother became the family's rebel, and she made it quite clear that she did not want to become *eine Hausfrau,* a housewife, but intended to become a hair dresser. Young Mathilde Maria (changed to Maria Mathilde when she became a US. citizen) was pretty and athletic, interested in all the latest fads: blond hair, modish hair styles, and pretty clothes.

As the threat of another war became more real, my mother and other young Germans found ways to escape their fears by going to neighborhood dances. At one of these socials, when she was only seventeen, Mathilde met an older man named Willy, who was twenty. They started dating, fell in love, and in a very short time, I happened — the classic unwanted pregnancy.

Back then, pregnancies outside of marriage were looked upon as shameful family tragedies, so my mother decided to keep hers a secret for as long as she could. But no secrets stay secrets for long, do they?

After three agonizing months, my mother's finally came out when one of her friends alerted the family, "Have you noticed something different about Mathilde these days?" Indeed, my grandmother had, and together with my grandfather and my aunt, they tearfully confronted her. It was painfully obvious she was no longer their "little" girl.

Years later, my mother told me what it was like for her at that time. "For three months I didn't tell anyone that I was pregnant. I was able to hide it well, but it was a terrible time for me. I felt miserable, helpless and desperate, and when I was alone in my room, I cried all the time."

Now that *I* was out of the bag, so to speak, the adults around Mother began to fret about what to do next. And, even though she was burdened by her own guilt and disgrace about the pregnancy, my young mother's wishes and feelings weren't considered at all.

I found out what happened next as she reluctantly went back to that dark time and spilled her guts, "You can't imagine how hard it was for me! A neighbor lady gave Oma a black potion to help me lose the baby, and I had to drink the bitter liquid for three days. It made me so sick."

But the abortion attempt didn't work, so the family turned to the next option: marriage. As she was forced to go along with Plan B, my mother knew it would shatter her dreams for the future. My Aunt Lisbeth acted as the negotiator between the two families. Faced with the news, my father said without any hesitation, *"Ich liebe Mathilde, ich liebe Familie. Wir heiraten.* I love Mathilde, I love family life. We'll get married." And so, in July of 1940, Mathilde and Willy got married. Three months later I was born.

Even though my father had already been drafted into the German army, he was granted a short leave so he could come home to greet me. Our home was on *Oberheidstrasse,* Over the Meadow Street, in the comfortable two-story house of my maternal grandparents where six of us lived under one roof. From what I've heard, Oma Maria and Opa Josef, Aunt Lisbeth and my three-year-old cousin Ilse, could not stop fussing over me from the minute my folks brought me home.

But it was war time, and everyone was forced to change. When people began to be taken away for no reason (or so it seemed), even their neighbors were too scared to question it. And, since no explanations were forthcoming, no

4

one knew what unspeakable fate awaited those who were whisked away. Even priests who spoke against the regime faced being arrested. In those impossibly frightening and difficult times, no one was safe.

My family disagreed with Hitler and rejected the Nazi Party but both my uncle and father had been drafted and sent off to the Russian front to fight a war that they did not want to fight. That left my Oma, Opa, Tante, my aunt, and Mutter to hold down the fort in *Muelheim-Ruhr,* Home by the Mill on the Ruhr River. Everyone had his hands full just trying to survive. Fortunately, my resourceful grandparents owned *ein Milchgeschaeft,* a dairy store, so they were able to barter with other shopkeepers and their own customers for many of the staples that were being rationed. My mother recalls that, "We were pretty lucky because we were able to trade our milk and butter for bread and meat. But we never shopped for our clothes during the war. We sewed or knitted everything."

My family stuck together somehow, and most of our physical needs got handled. But my emotional needs were completely ignored. After all, how could my mother, stuck with me and her shattered dreams, provide any real nurturing for her baby?

When she was six months pregnant, she'd been forced to attend a Nazi-sponsored class for future mothers. There, the nurse-instructors had been adamant about the best way to rear a child. "When it starts crying, don't pick it up. And if you handle your child just right — by spanking it — it will always obey you. As your child grows, all you'll have to do is look it in the eyes, and it will know what you want it to do or not to do. You will have a very obedient child."

Sure enough, my mother has always boasted that I hardly ever cried when I was a baby. And Lord knows I was obedient — until I wasn't, when I was around fourteen. I'm certain I'm not the only 60ish adult of German descent who's paid a very dear price for having been reared by parents using these strict and severe methods.

In her efforts to keep me quiet, she hardly ever used her bare hand, but chose instead to spank me hard with a wooden spoon. I believe now that my mother used such abusive methods because she truly believed I was her possession, and she only wanted to protect me from the war going on outside our door. But it ignited another kind of war — a conflict between mother and daughter. In retrospect, I believe I was only able to survive because of earth angels like my grandparents and my aunt, who nurtured me despite the war both inside and outside our home.

When I was still a baby, every night, all night long, the sirens howled. "Nights were not for rest," my mother sighed, as she recalled those times. "I never let you wear pajamas. I kept you dressed and ready in case we had to run to the shelters. As soon as the alarms began wailing, I had to wake you, grab you up and rush to get out of the house. We had a bunker in the backyard, but I preferred the more secure neighborhood shelter a few blocks away, even though it was sometimes scary getting there."

By 1942, when I was just two, the air attacks over our industrial Ruhr Valley got so bad that the women of my family joined many others in searching for a safer place to live. Many chose to take their children and flee to the countryside where farmers had been told by the government that they must exchange what food and shelter they had for the *Evakuierten,* evacuees' housework and farm labor.

Right away, Oma found the Meiers, near the village of *Schwalenberg* (Mountain of Swallows about 150 kilometers from Muelheim) who were willing to take us in. For the next three years, amongst the rolling hills and woods, we lived in relative calm. The farmer and his family treated us like one of his own, and there is no doubt in my mind that they probably saved our lives.

Over the years, my family stayed in touch with them, and in 1993, when my new husband and I were in Germany for our honeymoon, we visited the farmer's daughter, Elsbeth, who had married but was still living in the same area. She greeted me like a long lost sister. *"Ihr habt ja bei uns gelebt and wart wie Family.* You were like our own family when you lived with us."

Over coffee and cake, we talked about those dark days. Elsbeth, who is seven years my senior, reminisced about the many times she baby sat me and how we both loved to go off to the meadow to pick wild flowers.

Elsbeth and her husband, Fritz, reminded us that even though they had lived in a remote area, they, too, had been touched by the war's fury. Sadly, her brother, as well as other male relatives, never returned home after the war.

Fritz then shared a horrific incident he'd witnessed. "As the war was coming to an end, British fighter planes began to fly over this area in the dark of night. They were on their way to other parts of the country, but one night, as we listened to the familiar roars overhead, it was obvious that one of the little planes was having engine problems. We all listened in horror as it hurtled through the nearby woods and crashed. The next morning, a group of us, still in shock, rushed to the crash site. What greeted us were airplane parts scattered all through the winter woods and then we spotted a man in uniform dangling from a tree." With a faraway look in his eyes and sorrow in his voice, Fritz concluded, "I can still see that British pilot in my mind as though it all happened yesterday." As he spoke, I remembered my connection to that sad tale. The tragic story of the pilot in the tree had been the talk of the town and had filled my three-year-old mind with terrible, haunting images for a long time.

When I was four, another incident happened nearby that shook me to my core. According to Mami, "Just a few days before the war was over, American tankers rolled into *Schwalenberg*, and the troops inside them went about systematically shooting the few German soldiers who were still trying to protect our little town."

"Early the next morning, you and I hurried to *Brakelsieg*, the tiny village next to *Schwalenberg*, to see Tante Lisbeth and Ilse. As we frantically ran down the road connecting the two villages, I spotted piles of German soldiers' corpses lining the ditches. Right away I told you not to look in that direction, but I don't know if it was soon enough. Even if you did get a glimpse of that dreadful sight, I believed that you didn't really know what was going on." Mami, I did see. And oh, how wrong you were!

It was most healing for me to go back to *Schwalenberg* for some closure. Renewing my friendship with Elsbeth warmed my heart and seeing the now-peaceful countryside helped change the landscape of my scarred mind.

On the same 1993 trip to Germany, my husband and I also visited the rebuilt city of my birth. We stayed at a small farmhouse converted into a hotel which was located only three blocks from my neighborhood on *Oberheidstrasse*. There I was able to release many of the fear-filled images I had long carried deep inside of me.

Opa lived through much terror there while the women and children of our family were living in *Schwalenberg's* relative safety. Bombs destroyed many houses in our old neighborhood in *Muelheim*, killing many friends and neighbors. Even though most of these bombs (appropriately called "blockbusters") were intended for weapon factories or other strategic targets, they often missed their marks.

One such stray bomb exploded half a block away from my grandparents' house. When news of how bodies and parts of bodies were found in the rubble of homes and in the streets, my grandmother, aunt and mother went into hysterics, and I overheard everything. They thought I wasn't old enough to feel any of their pain and fear, but I was.

One day in the spring of 1944, the news was even worse: my grandparents' home had been hit. It was a miracle my grandfather wasn't harmed.

Even though we hadn't been there, Opa's account of what happened made us know how close he'd come to being killed. On that nightmare of a night, he did what he usually did — he ran for the backyard bunker as soon as he heard the air raid sirens begin. There, Opa held the shelter door ajar as his neighbors hurried to get inside.

However, before he could secure the door, he heard a whoosh and felt it slam on top of him from the force of the bomb's impact. Opa knew his house had taken a hit, and he had no choice but to come out and watch while it burned to the ground. Indeed, the next morning all that remained were the steps leading up to what had been the front door and a small portion of the bathroom wall with the sink still attached. The rest of his home of fifteen years was a pile of rubble.

Our neighbors' house had been hit, too, and their little daughter, who was my age, was killed in the explosion. For a long time after that, my mother repeated the story of how my family had to listen to her grieving parents bemoan, "Why did Bettina live and our little Brigitte die?"

Forty years later, as my husband and I stood on the spot where our house had once been, I recalled that time and many other times during the brutal war when I heard my mother sob over the loss of friends and relatives, including her beloved Aunt Paula who, with her daughter Agathe, had been crushed by a bomb.

As my husband held me in the comfort of his arms, I now felt safe to cry, too, and out loud, bringing solace at last to little Bettina. *She* had witnessed everything, but had been forced to bury her tears deep in the bunker of her mind.

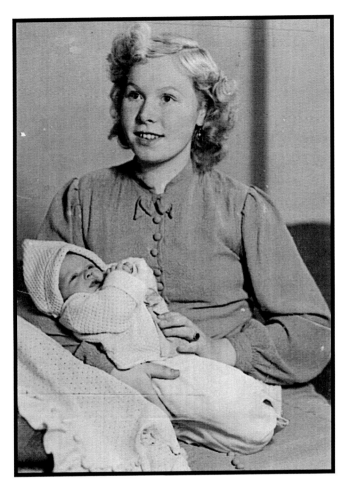

1940 – Young Mother Mathilde with Baby Bettina

**1941 – Maternal Grandparents and one year old
Bettina**

Cousin Ilse with Bettina in Carriage

Home on Oberheid Street –Bombed in 1944

Chapter 2

Life in the Ruins

Soon after the war ended in August of 1945, our little group of evacuees said *Aufwiedersehen* to our adopted farm family and returned to bombed-out Mülheim to the unknown and the rebuilding of our lives.

The first thing to tackle was where we would all be living. Tante Lisbeth and Ilse went to live with Uncle Fritz who, luckily, had returned safely from the war and had already found a tiny apartment nearby for the three of them to live in.

Since Mami and I had no place to go, we once again moved in with my maternal grandparents. This time it was *ein Behilfsheim* (literally, a home of help) — the temporary shelter that Opa Josef and some neighbors had quickly put up right behind the rubble of the old house.

This small, rectangular concrete block structure had a narrow entry way where we neatly lined up our shoes. Against the back wall, pantry shelves hid behind a flowered curtain. To the right, a door led to the kitchen/living area, a room dominated by the coal-burning stove and its towering pipe. That stove provided the only heat for our little house and a warm central area for all our family activities. An old fashioned brown velvet sofa and a fringed floor lamp took up the left wall. In front of the sofa was an all-purpose table where everyone gathered to prepare food, eat and talk.

But my favorite piece of furniture in that overcrowded room was the easy chair that occupied the place of honor next to the big table. It was Opa's chair and that's where I used to crawl up into his lap to tickle his beloved bald head while he blissfully smoked his pipe.

This patient, soft-spoken man and my sweet Oma Maria worried all the time about how skinny I was, so they both came up with clever ways to deal with my situation. Oma knit thick knee-high socks for me to wear so my legs would look bigger. Opa covered thick slices of fresh bread with butter and yummy homemade jam, cut them in bite-size pieces, then coaxed me to eat them one by one. I still like to prepare this snack for myself and enjoy it more, knowing there's always enough.

I often accompanied Opa on his important *errands,* one of which was to go to the racetrack. There, he would let me advise him on which horses to bet. I always chose a white or silver one. Then off we'd go to the window where he'd give me his few extra *Pfennige t*o place a bet on our *sure winner.*

Every night, Opa tucked me into bed in the back room. In the winter, that room was like an icebox, but both my grandparents worked in tandem to make sure my feet were warm. First, Oma would warm a brick in the stove; then Opa would wrap it in a towel and tuck it under my covers at the foot of the bed. It was then he would talk to me about God and how powerful he thought God was because, after all, He had put the sun, the moon and all the stars in the sky. Looking back at those troubled times, I think he was trying to convince himself as well as me that God still cared about us. Sometimes he would sing German folk songs to me and, just as I was drifting off to sleep, he'd hum Brahms' Lullaby, a song which still brings tears to my eyes every time I hear it.

Each time Mother was busy helping in the milk store or out having fun with her friends, Oma took me under her wing. Often, that would mean spending time with her in her spotless kitchen. There, she would scurry about, wearing a flowery apron that barely fit over her ample tummy, preparing the meals she knew her family loved. As far as I was concerned, Oma was the best cook in the world!

Sunday meals were extra special, especially since meat was still in short supply. Somehow, she always managed to get enough to make a delicious *Braten,* roast, accompanied by potatoes, gravy and vegetables. Whenever Oma cooked, our cramped living quarters quickly filled with the aromas of her efforts. Those smells would linger long after we'd finished eating and the dishes were done. And that's when I'd snuggle up in her still-aproned lap to get as many of her hugs as I could until it was time to go to bed.

And Oma was also the best baker. I always felt extra special when she would let me be her helper. I can't remember ever passing up the chance to stir whatever she was making, because I knew I would be allowed to clean out the last little bits of the sweet, raw batter from the heavy mixing bowl. I did a first-class licking job to finish off the spoon while the cookies or cake she prepared baked in the oven

Another fun activity we'd do together was go to the cemetery each month to tend to Oma's first husband's grave site. We'd pull weeds or rake leaves or do whatever she thought needed to be done, and then, depending on what time of year it was, we'd plant something or place a little bouquet of flowers near the headstone. Each time when we'd finish, she would become quiet and sometimes cry a little bit. Then she'd ask me to pray with her, which I willingly did even though I didn't really understand why she was so sad.

Not far from the cemetery was St. Barbara's Church, a small structure that replaced the original building which had been destroyed by bombs during the war. Every Sunday, Oma took me with her to Mass, but I never felt very uplifted there because it was almost always freezing inside, dark and dreary and filled with sad-looking old women in their shabby coats, bundled up against the cold just like me. What did make me feel good was when Oma talked about her love for Jesus and how she knew He was listening to our prayers.

Oma and Opa weren't able to devote all their time to

me, and besides, I sometimes liked to play by myself. But right after the war, playtime was different because toys were still hard to come by. I clung to the only two I had — a teddy bear and one doll, *meine Puppe,* which I loved and could play with for hours even though she had peeling painted hair and eyes and only one shabby dress.

In my neighborhood, not only had most of my playmates disappeared, but there was only one playground — the bombed out houses that dotted our block. Sometimes I'd pretend that everything was as it had been — that every one of the nice homes, with their lovely furniture and friendly families, welcomed me as I romped around. But I often learned the hard way just how much everything had changed and that my imaginary world was just that. Because, even though I was very careful as I climbed up and down and around the rubble, I suffered lots of scratched knees and elbows that had to be tended to when I got home.

About a year after we'd returned to *Muelheim*, I started school. That first day, after somehow scraping together the supplies I needed, my mother proudly walked her frightened little six-year-old *kleine* Bettina into the *Schildberg* School. My life changed drastically on this day because not only did I now have children to relate to after being surrounded by adults for so long, but most importantly, I began my new life of learning. It took me no time at all to find out how much I enjoyed learning to read, write and draw. Above all, I realized from the start that school was a safe place for me, a welcome refuge from my mother's raging and spanking.

There was one more reason that school meant so much to me. For as long as I could remember, my mother had spent as little quality time with me as she could get away with. But now, with the advent of school, she tried her best to keep me motivated and praised me when I did well — something I had craved because I had so little from her.

On most Sundays and holidays, Mutter and I visited the Zendel family: my dear Aunt Lisbeth, Onkel Fritz, and Cousin Ilse who didn't live very far from us. I loved going there because, just like she'd done when we'd all lived in the country, my aunt fussed over me and showered me with love from the moment I walked into her home.

Those visits also gave Ilse and me the chance to play together like sisters, even though she is three years my senior, and to cement the bond we enjoy to this day. I loved to go 'shopping' in Ilse's closet because it was overflowing with pretty clothes that Aunt Lisbeth had sewn for her and that would later become mine. I constantly pestered her about certain dresses, hoping that she would tire of them sooner rather than later.

Every time I went over to Ilse's and saw her father, it made me wonder *Wo ist mein Vater?* Where is my father? I'd been told that he was a prisoner of war, and I guessed that really wasn't his fault — a fact that didn't help me accept why he couldn't be there to love me.

I was also confused whenever my mother spoke about my father because, though everyone else always spoke highly of him, she always said, "Your father's a nice man but I could have done much better. I think he probably got me pregnant on purpose because he knew I was a good catch."

Imagine my surprise when, one day in the winter of 1947 I arrived home from school to hear the news that my father was on his way home to *Muelheim.* Without stopping her housework for a second, Oma told me, "Your Vater is finally coming back from the war. He'll be here soon!"

Most of the adult members of my family were excited about his return but mother was sending me mixed messages. I had mixed emotions. How could my little heart be happy to see the person who supposedly made my mother so *un*happy? Of course, I was curious to see this man, whom I'd been told to call *Pappi,* but I was frightened at the same time because

22

he had essentially been a stranger to me until now.

Finally, the day of the homecoming was upon us. Oma spent the entire day preparing a huge dinner that included *Sauerbraten* roast and *Buttercreme Torte* cake.

That evening, just after dark, I heard my mother call out, "There's someone at the door! He's here!"

As far as I was concerned, that was my signal to scamper to my hiding place under the table. There I watched first my mother, then both my grandparents embrace the unshaven uniformed man who was standing in our doorway looking very exhausted.

But, in the midst of all the hugging, I heard this stranger say, "*Wo ist denn unsere kleine Bettina?* Where is our little Bettina?"

My mother spotted me cowering under the table. She walked over, leaned down and said, "Come out and say hello to your *Vater.*"

And there he was, right next to her, saying, "*Da bist Du ja!* Oh, there you are!"

Slightly embarrassed, I slowly crawled out from under the table and got an awkward hug from my now-very-real father. Even though the situation was still a little strained, everything seemed okay.

As I listened closely to everyone talking that evening, I learned that it was indeed a miracle that Willy had survived the war. Not only had he lived through several harsh Russian winters but also survived after he'd at one point gotten down to only eighty pounds from starvation and internal bleeding. And then in 1945, on the very day the war had been declared over, his division had been captured in Yugoslavia, and he'd been detained for an additional two years. In the town where he and his fellow soldiers were imprisoned, a doctor decided to build a makeshift hospital. When the man found out that Willy was a plumber, he asked him to help with the construction. To hear my father tell it, it was his friendship with this doctor that kept him from being locked up, hurt or even dying during those two long years. It was this medical man's recommendation that had finally given him his freedom.

But for the most part, my father kept his wartime stories to himself, including the horror story about how at one point, he and his starving buddies had made the grim decision to dig up a dead horse and consume it in a desperate attempt to sustain themselves for another few days. So much did my father want to forget that hideous part of his past, that he didn't share this episode with me until just a few years ago.

With the passage of time, I slowly adjusted to having *Vater* in our family system. Even though our living quarters were now more cramped than ever, it was good to have an additional strong man to bring home the sacks full of potatoes, which were our main stay at the time. Just a day or two after he came home, he left in the dark of the night to catch a train to the countryside where he joined other foragers scrounging for leftovers in the already harvested fields.

While he scavenged for food, *Vater* also kept his eyes open for a real job. And thanks to the Marshall Plan, the United States' monetary assistance for the reconstruction of Europe, he quickly found work. Once again his skills served him well because they enabled him to partner with a local architect and start a plumbing and heating company.

The business did well enough so that after only six months, father was able to move his little family. We moved to a tiny walk-up apartment in a tenement neighborhood full of ghostly ruins located on *Mellinghofer Strasse,* Mellinghofer Street, not very far from my grandparent's home.

Our two room apartment on the third floor had only one sink situated in the kitchen. Taking a bath meant boiling water on our gas stove to fill the big iron tub that had been dragged to its place of honor in the middle of the floor. Also, the three of us had to share the water closet (toilet), located half a flight below us, with some other tenants of the building.

Even as my physical world improved a little, the world of my emotions spiraled downward. My parents spent almost all their waking hours arguing about everything under the sun and paid very little attention to me. Their rages scared me so much that I ran and hid in the bedroom where I prayed to God that the yelling would stop. But it didn't. Nor did my mother's game of getting me to side with her against Vater or, even more frightening, the one where she'd convince him to turn against me. I missed my grandparents so much, and without them under the same roof as me, I felt more abandoned than ever, but I never let my feelings show.

My father's perception of me back then goes like this: "Bettina, you were such a good girl, so quiet. You never said very much." How could he know that my mother had done such a good job of silencing my little spirit, that I had been too terrified to tell him what was bothering me. How could he know that I'd been forbidden to let him know how much I needed his help? So, because he thought that she'd done such a good job while he'd been gone, he passively let my mother be the one responsible for my upbringing. However, that allowed the abuse to continue.

How did I survive? One escape was my passion for learning. I somehow continued to excel at school.

My other respite came from the Catholic Church and especially the events in the spring of 1948 leading to and including the day of my First Communion. Not only was I happy about receiving Jesus into my heart, but I was also delighted about the fact that the entire celebration centered around me for a change.

Well in advance of that important day, *Mutter* and

Oma began to prepare for a sit-down luncheon. Both my paternal and maternal grandparents were coming, along with Onkel Friedel, my father's brother (who had been designated as my godfather), his wife and their son, my nine year old cousin, *Friedel.* My dear Tante Lisbeth (who was my newly appointed godmother) was coming with Ilse.

Of course, I needed a new outfit for my special day. Even though the shops were still understocked, Mother and I did manage to find a pretty white coat, white dress and stockings, as well as a pair of shiny black patent leather oxfords for me to wear. To complete the ensemble, we bought a crown of small make-believe white roses to sit atop my head.

On the morning of the service, mother fussed over me much more than usual, curling my hair into sweet ringlets instead of putting it in its everyday braids. She wanted to make sure I looked just right for all the curious eyes that awaited us at the church. No matter what her motives were, for a change I felt really good.

Once we got to Saint Barbara's Church, I joined the other boys and girls in the front pews and began to concentrate on receiving Jesus into my life. I was hoping that I would feel less fearful of the God I didn't understand and who seemed to punish us so much.

I also loved all the activities after the Mass. My entire entourage gathered around me, their star, and lavished me with praise. Later on, we all met in our tiny living quarters and sat at the beautiful luncheon table decorated with flowers, candles and our best china. I still have many of the photographs taken that day, including one of the entire family standing in the garden, ignoring the ruins all around. And everyone seemed to be focused on me and my bright future.

Only two nights later, the flames of my happiness were extinguished when my mother came to my bed sobbing.

As she shook me awake she said, "Bettina, you have to stay strong. Oma always told me she would be ready to leave in peace after your First Communion and that is what she has done. Tonight, Oma had a heart attack and died."

Even though I was in total disbelief, I followed my mother's instructions and fumbled into my clothes. When dawn broke that cold, late spring morning, she and I forlornly began the two mile hike up the hillside road that led to the old *Behilfsheim,* their two room shelter.

When we finally got there, everything seemed so strange, so different, because Oma was not at her usual place in front of the stove. With tears streaming down my cheeks, I ran over to Opa who was sitting in his rocker with his head down on his chest. "Please, please tell me it's not true!" I screamed.

"*Sie ist jestzt im Himmel, Schaetzchen.* She's gone to heaven, my precious one," he moaned as he lifted me up and hugged me. But no matter what he said or did, he couldn't console me, and we sobbed together.

A few minutes later, my Aunt Lisbeth tried to calm me down by reminding me how much Oma had suffered with her recent strokes. She hugged me and said, "Oma doesn't hurt anymore, *Bettinalein.* And she's much happier because now she's in heaven with God."

But all I could think of was that death had taken away my one source of comfort— my safety net. I didn't understand how she could possibly be happier away from me!

After what seemed like forever, my aunt (who looked as if she he'd cried for days) asked, "Would you like to see your Oma one more time, Bettina? She is lying in bed and looks like she's just asleep."

The thought of looking at her hadn't even occurred to me, but I reluctantly took my aunt's hand and bravely walked

27

into the bedroom with her.

There she was lying on her back in one of her prettiest nightgowns, her eyes closed and her hands folded as if in prayer. She looked quite content and very much at peace. As my little body shook with even more sobs, I said, "*Ich liebe Dich, Oma.* I love you. *Aufwidersehen!*"

Three days later, everyone who knew her gathered for a beautiful funeral, and she was put to her final rest in the same place where she and I had spent so many happy hours.

For a long time after that day, I cried a lot and continued to hurt in my own quiet way. I tried to get back into life, but without Oma, I felt so lost.

1945 – Bettina with Teddy

**Celebrating Holy Communion with
Family in midst of Ruins**

Bettina with Paternal Grandparents

Chapter 3

AUF WIEDERSEHEN

Since I had just transferred to Middle School, one that was a little more challenging, I really threw myself into my schoolwork after Oma died. But the other thing that made my life a little more bearable was that Opa came to live with us in our little apartment on *Mellinghofer Strasse*. So, for a while, life was okay.

However, by 1950, two years after Oma's death, I was thrown into shock again when my mother told me she wanted the three of us to leave Germany and move to America. She tried to tell me what a big, beautiful country it was and that the people were much friendlier there. But, I was confused about how leaving my friends and everything familiar could make me happy.

Of course, I didn't really have any say in the decision making process. And, in the end, neither did my *Vater*. For months after *Mutter* let us in on her secret of her long time desire to move to America, she did her best to convince him that the move was in our best interest. She used reasoning such as, "There's always a chance of another war here, but not over there. In war time, soldiers rape women, and I don't want our Bettina to have to go through that." All the while *Mutter* was making arrangements for our milk store to be given to her cousin who in turn would care for Opa.

When I complained that I'd miss him and our relatives, she countered with, "All they ever do is show off, besides we really don't need them or anybody here." After a while, I just gave up and pretended to like her idea. Inside I remained unconvinced and sad.

My father was opposed to the idea, too, because he

was happy right where he was. Being back home with all his loved ones was ideal. Plus, he also knew that his company had possibilities of being very, very successful and rightfully hated to abandon it.

In the end, my mother played her trump card. "Well, if you won't go with us, I'll just take Bettina and we'll go without you!" That's when my father gave up, and preparations began in earnest for the move.

They made applications to emigrate both to Canada and the United States. Canada was the country that opened its doors first. So, we passed our required physical exams and waited for our departure date. Even though my parents got to have farewell parties with their friends, Mother told me I had to keep our plan a secret. I couldn't really say good bye to any of mine.

I guess it was tough for *Mutter* to leave Opa because, in no uncertain terms, she said that none of us were to say goodbye to him. But since he lived under the same roof, it wasn't hard for him to know the exact date of our departure.

During our last night home, as I pretended to be sound asleep, Opa's shadowy figure appeared at my bedside. He knelt down and whispered, "*Ich liebe Dich und werde immer an Dich denken.* I love you and I will always think about you." I somehow managed to keep my eyes shut tight, but the minute I sensed that he was gone, I began to cry silently and choked back my tears. Those were the last words my grandfather spoke to me because he died ten years later, a long time before we'd go to Germany to visit.

At day break, *Vater* carried our suitcases down the stairs to the taxi that was waiting to take us to the station. There, we boarded the train to the port city of Bremen. As the country side passed by in a blur outside the train's window, my mind and heart blurred too with mixed emotions.

Was I to feel sad about leaving or excited about the adventures that awaited me?

When we finally got to Bremen after a day-long train ride, we were met by representatives from our ship. They informed us that we probably wouldn't be sailing for two days because many of the passengers hadn't arrived yet. They showed us the way to the primitive dorm where they had arranged to put us up.

As it happened, our temporary housing was located right next to the city's small airport where some planes left over from the war were hangared. *Vater's* curiosity was piqued. So, the next morning while we were still sleeping, he got up and went over there to explore. In no time at all, he found a pilot that was willing to take him up.

Mutter and I were leisurely getting dressed when he returned, his face just beaming. "You'll never guess what I've been doing! I just went up for an airplane ride and, wow, was it exciting to see the ground from way up there!" he exclaimed.

"And guess what, Bettina? The pilot is going up again in just a little while and he told me he'd take you up with him if you want to go."

"*Fliegen? Dafuer habe ich aber angst.* Fly? I'm too scared to do that!" was my much stunned and mumbled reaction.

My father noticed my hesitation and continued, "I've never been up there before either, *Schaetzchen*, little treasure. But look! I came down safe and here I am in one piece. It felt really good! It'll be lots of fun and I know you'll be so glad you went once you're up there."

His enthusiasm immediately rubbed off on my ever adventurous mother, and before I could think about it much more she, too, began to coax me to go for it. Finally, I whispered, "*Ja, ich moechte auch fliegen.* Yes, I'd like to fly, too."

So, before I had time to change my mind, my parents walked me over to the little airport where the pilot greeted me. "*Da ist ja das kleine Maedchen! Ihr habt ja eine grosse Reise vor Euch!* Ah, there's the little girl! You sure have a big trip ahead of you!" His friendliness comforted me about the imminent trip into the sky.

"*Alles ist vertig. Kommst Du mit?* All's ready to go. Are you ready to come along?"

Even though I was committed now, I nodded only halfheartedly as I stared at the single engine plane looming on the tarmac. It seemed very similar to the ones I'd been so afraid of during the war. But I had to admit that after the war, when I'd hear and see airplanes rumbling overhead, I would often wonder, "*Wie fuehlt man sich so hoch zu sein ueber Alles?* I wonder what it would feel like to be high above everything?" I knew I would have my answer then and there.

Both my parents looked on proudly and began to wave as the pilot helped me get onto the plane, into my seat and buckled up. As for me, my insides were shaking so hard that I was barely able to wave back at my folks.

Just after Herr Pilot revved up the engine, we began roaring and rocking down the runway. I held my breath as I felt the plane's power surge through my entire body as we began to lift off and climb through the air.

I must say I felt surprisingly secure floating through the air, even though we were bouncing around in the clouds a little bit. And, as I pressed my nose against the tiny window, I couldn't believe what was happening right before my eyes. Everything was getting smaller and smaller, yet I could see so *much more!* The field's shapes and colors melted into one big design. Trees bordering the farmland looked liked seams holding the landscape together. Villages became clusters of red slate rooftops nestled beside the winding threads that I knew were roads. I loved the expanded view I was getting from up in the air and felt more free than I had ever been before in my whole life! Even when we bounced through some more clouds, I was not scared.

But flying was a pretty fast business, and before I knew it, we had made our thrilling though uneventful descent. We were back on solid ground in the hangar and the plane's engine had come to a grinding halt.

I crawled to the plane's door, still dizzy and very quiet. There I was met by my father. *"War das nicht schoen!* Wasn't that great!" It was not a question; it was a statement of fact. And I had to agree with him. Even though I was back down on earth, my heart was still up in the air.

Father and I thanked the friendly pilot for giving us our first plane ride. I had no idea God would bless me with a career that would give me so many instant replays of that magic moment.

Passport Photos - We were asked not to smile!

Father

Mother

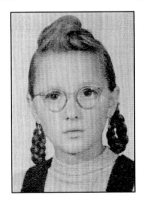

Bettina

Bettina's First Day Going to Middle School

1951 – Goodbye to my home city of Mülheim

Chapter 4

Hello "New World"

Two days later we woke up early on a very cool and foggy summer morning. We hurriedly got ready for the next part of our journey — our voyage overseas.

As we reached the dock, Mutter explained to me that you could tell how big a ship was by the number of smokestacks it had. She said the more smokestacks, the larger the ship. So I looked with awe upon the Canberra, our Greek passenger liner, as it sat at anchor right in front of us. And even though I could see only one smokestack looming high above, that vessel still appeared gigantic to my 10 year old eyes.

Mutter, Vater and I carefully climbed up the metal gangplank and rushed right over to the railing to join the other passengers who were frantically waving to everyone on the dock. But our little family wasn't necessarily waving goodbye to the strangers below. Our gestures were waves of "Auf Wiedersehen zu unsere Heimat — Farewell to our homeland, until we see you again."

Before long, we heard the ship's hollow voiced horns and felt her vibrations as she began chugging out of the little port of Bremen with her cargo of brave souls aboard — each one in search of a new home. For hours, the huge ship gently rocked us as Germany's distant shoreline slowly disappeared behind us. Meanwhile, my parents and I stepped below to check out our tiny, windowless cabin located on the ship's lowest deck. Just one look at this chicken coop sized room gave us all the incentive we needed to spend most of our time on the top deck for the duration of our three-week voyage.

Not long into the journey, the ship's small dining room became my parents' favorite place, not only to eat, but also to meet the other passengers. Many were from Eastern Europe and were still talking about how they lost their homes and so much more during the war, yet now they were also looking hopefully to the future. My parents befriended one couple who had a 17 year old daughter named Christa. Since there were very few children my age on board, she and I became buddies as well.

Just a few days after setting out, we encountered rough seas. My parents were lucky; they seemed to take all the tossing about quite well. I, on the other hand, had to stay below deck where Mutter and *Vater* took turns bringing me dry rolls — the only thing that seemed to settle my poor little tummy.

But each time the seas calmed, I scampered up top for some fresh air and to join everyone in the bustling dining room. Whenever the weather would allow, Christa and I explored the ship, or I just sat alone on a lounge chair and stared out at the endless ocean. That particular activity was most soothing because it gave me a break from everything that was cluttering my mind — homesickness for Germany and anxiety about what lay ahead.

About two weeks into our voyage, crewmen told everyone to gather at once at the lifeboat station. Only after we had assembled with concern on our faces were we told that it was only a drill. Then they handed each of us a life vest and proceeded to teach us what to do just in case.

After three seemingly endless weeks, we knew our days of living aboard the Canberra were almost over because the shoreline of Canada came into view at last. But that day, July 1st, happened to be her Independence Day — *Dominion Day* — and it soon became clear that none of us were getting off the boat just yet. Because of the national holiday, no one was on the job to check our papers. They all had the day off!

So we were forced to remain on the ship for one more uncomfortable night. The next morning, we officially entered Canada and passed through Immigration. But we still weren't allowed to disembark until completing the last leg down the St. Lawrence River to our final destination, the city of Montreal.

Once we docked, pandemonium reigned with people shoving each other aside to be among the first to set foot on their New World's soil. But our family could only watch as some of our fellow passengers were met by happy relatives, because we knew no one. If someone on the ship hadn't given us the name of a local German church group that helped people like us, arriving with no knowledge of Canada's language or customs, we would've been at a total loss about what to do.

It didn't take us long to locate these kind folks on the bustling dock, and the minute we approached them, they welcomed us with open arms. Then they took us to a nearby coffee shop and treated us to refreshments. That's when I had my first 7-Up ever, and it was just that— refreshing. These people were full of encouraging words and, not only that, encouraging actions. Much to our amazement, they were able to help us find an apartment that same day. Later that afternoon, they took us and our meager belongings to yet another new neighborhood.

As the sun was about to set on that steamy, stifling summer day, we stopped in front of what seemed like an endless row of buildings. On the second floor of one of them, our unfurnished place awaited us. We trudged up the stairs and opened what we thought was a door to just another tenement apartment. But, as we crossed its threshold, we couldn't believe our eyes! It was so spacious! Before us we could see a huge combination kitchen/living room and the other doors leading to two big bedrooms. But the biggest surprise awaited us at the end of the hallway. There, right in our apartment, was a bathroom that housed both a tub and a toilet! What a contrast to our facility-less living space we had endured in the old country! Since we had left most of our belongings behind in Germany, that first night and for several weeks thereafter we slept atop blankets on the floor. And, for the first few months, orange crates served as our only furniture. But it didn't seem to matter — we all felt better than we had in a long time. Oh, how very much our lifestyle had improved in just one month's time! Yes, everything was new and strange, but it was so much bigger and better and, best of all, there were no bombed out buildings in sight! Within a week, the city's German community helped my father find a job. They even got one for my mother who began sewing in a sweatshop. Although the work left her exhausted, each day on her way home, she loved shopping amidst the huge variety offered at every grocery store. Almost every evening, she'd bring her purchases home and then throw herself into cooking a good meal for her family.

I was lucky we had gotten to Canada during the summer because it gave me the chance to connect with some of the neighborhood kids outside the confines of school. One nice afternoon I watched two little girls playing on the sidewalk with some thin, multi-colored sticks. One of them kept on smiling at me and waving for me to come over. I don't know how, but after a few minutes, I summoned up the courage to do so.

The little girl who waved tried to tell me in French that her name was Monique. When she noticed my puzzled look, she switched to the few English words she knew. But somehow, even though I'd only taken one year of basic English, I was able to communicate that I spoke only German. Again, this pretty little girl with black, curly hair and dark brown eyes smiled and began as best she could to explain the game of Pickup Sticks to me without using many words at all.

That first day, Monique and I connected through the universal language of smiles and gestures. And over the summer, we worked on improving talking skills and solidifying our friendship. Oh, I was so happy that she had put out the welcome mat for me and that I had someone I could call my friend.

Before long, summer was almost over, and it was time to make arrangements for me to attend school. My parents were faced with the choice of enrolling me in a French or English speaking school. We all concluded that it would be best for me to try the latter, hoping that the English I'd learned in Germany would be enough to help me start my education in Canada.

After the school finished processing my registration information, they made the decision to place me in the third grade, rather than the fifth grade, where I would have been in a German school. My parents were assured that this decision for placement was only temporary and that, as soon as I passed all the tests, I would be advanced.

When school started, I was assigned to a desk in back of the room because I was the tallest and oldest one in the

class. That made me feel so awkward and very much like the foreigner that I was. From the start of the term, learning spelling, vocabulary and grammar was quite challenging for me. On the other hand, I really loved my math classes and was able to breeze right through them with ease. I felt very proud of myself because I quickly mastered enough English skills to be promoted from third grade to fourth. By the end of the school year, I ended up in the fifth grade. With all that grade changing, it was very hard for me to feel any sense of belonging or to form lasting friendships with my classmates. So this little German immigrant continued to feel like an outsider navigating a lonesome solo flight through life.

But, once again, my 'little girl' found some solace within the church. St. Barbara's was its name, the same as my old church in *Mülheim*. My parents' habit of making excuses for not going to church with me, just like they had done in the old country, continued — something about needing their rest after their hard working week. They let me walk the three short blocks from our apartment to the church by myself. The Latin Mass and familiar hymns, such as *Grosser Gott Wir Loben Dich* How Great Thou Art, reminded me of home. I really enjoyed listening to the priest deliver sermons in his somewhat unfamiliar German dialect. But I would still be jealous of the other children sitting in our special section, because they were there with their families. After the service, when I saw them gathered outside planning their afternoon fun activities, I got sad all over again because I knew really all I had to look forward to was returning to our sparsely furnished apartment where I would be forced to listen to my parents' constant bickering for the rest of the day. I couldn't wait to escape back to school on Monday mornings.

Not that I didn't have a few good times. Since my folks wanted to get to know our new city better, we'd sometimes go on Sunday excursions to nearby parks or take a train out to the beautiful Quebec countryside, where we'd partake of a yummy picnic my mother had prepared.

In the wintertime, I looked forward to trekking to the outdoor ice skating rink in Mt. Royal Park. There, I'd put on the new figure skates my parents had bought me and glide around the rink to the rhythm of the music blaring from the speakers. At first I needed help just to stay upright, but after awhile, I actually got pretty good at it. The only thing that bothered me was that I had to skate alone while I watched the other kids and adults happily skating in pairs.

About three months after we'd moved into our second story apartment, a German widow, Mrs. Heberle, and her three daughters moved in below us. Two of the girls were in their early twenties, and one was my age. Needless to say, our families quickly became friends. Even though Rosie and I attended different schools, we played together a lot.

For at least six months, our two families exchanged frequent dinner visits, but all too soon, our closeness came to an abrupt end. When Mutter began to suspect that the adult sisters were being much too friendly with my father and he with them, she insisted that we stop having anything to do with them. I was no longer allowed to spend any time with my little friend that had nothing to do with the adults.

Eight months after mother began working at the sweatshop, she decided that it was too hard for her, so she changed jobs and became a cleaning lady for several rich suburban housewives. Occasionally, she'd let me go with her to their elegant homes. I'd never been in such mansions or seen such beautiful furnishings, so I behaved myself, stayed out of her way and sat quietly coloring most of the day. Since we were in need of everything to furnish our apartment, mother was always grateful for the castoffs that her employers often gave us.

But just as it seemed that we had settled into our new way of life, my mother brought it to a screeching halt. After eighteen months in Montreal, she decided it was time to make another move.

After church one Sunday, she informed me, "Bettina, guess what? We're leaving Montreal and going to Edmonton!"

I was so upset at the thought of moving again that all I could do was shriek, "Leave Montreal! Why?"

"Your father has been promised a job at an oil refinery where he'll earn three times the pay he's making here," she explained matter-of-factly.

It didn't make any difference to her that I was in the middle of sixth grade, and I didn't want to separate from the few friends I'd managed to make. We were going, and that was that. So I helped pack up the things I was told I could take with me, said my sad goodbyes and reluctantly prepared to leave my first North American home. And once again, I was anxious about what the future would hold.

**1951 in Bremen. Part of saying
goodbye to Germany**

1951 – Our overseas vessel Canberra

Summer of 1951 in Montreal
Monique (left) Bettina (right)

Montréal 1952 –Adopting New Customs

Chapter 5

Move Across Canada

In April of 1953, only twenty months after leaving Germany, we once again sold or gave away whatever we could of our meager possessions and set out on our journey east to west, across the vast expanse of Canada. This time our mode of transportation wasn't an ocean liner but a dark blue, 2 door, 1949 Ford coupe that my father had been able to buy with the little money he had saved.

And once again, for me, the whole process was a mixture of confusion and anticipation. I was barely able to accept that we were moving again, but I was also curious about what the next place would be like for me. So I just crawled into the back seat of that car and settled in for the long, long ride.

It was memorable, to say the least, considering the language barrier, all the snow (even in April) and some unplanned events.

One afternoon, as we were driving along the icy roads amidst the breathtaking winter landscapes, our whole family saw what we thought was a mirage. As my father slowed the car, we thought we were looking at two deer, one large and one small. But what we really saw was a mother elk and her little one, standing like statues in the middle of the road.

My father responded at once and was able to bring the car to a complete stop very close to where they stood. He turned off the engine. So there we sat, in a freezing five minute standoff that seemed to last forever, until the four legged mother and child finally decided to amble off into the woods. Relieved that he'd avoided what could have been a tragedy, my father quickly started the car, and we too were once again on our way.

What *I* couldn't avoid was listening to my parents' constant fighting over how to drive and what roads to take. It was almost impossible to keep from letting their stress become my stress, but I huddled in the back seat and tried to devise ways to shut out the angry voices. Hour upon hour, I concentrated on staring out the car at the beautiful countryside passing by. Or, I read and reread the comic books that I had remembered to bring along, all the while silently praying we would make it to Edmonton in one piece. Somehow we did.

Once again my parents connected with the German community, and once again they were able to help us find a place to call home in the new city. A couple who owned a little grocery store suggested we go see a retired Polish widower who owned and lived in a two-story house near their establishment. After meeting with my parents, Mr. Novak decided to rent his downstairs apartment to us. Even though it was much smaller than the place we had lived in in Montreal, my folks decided that it was pleasant enough and would do until they were able to afford something better.

Within a week, as anticipated, my father reported to his better paying oil refinery job. But, since the school year was almost over by the time we got to Alberta, it didn't make sense for me to enroll until the fall.

Mother, who'd decided not to go to work, spent her time decorating the apartment and socializing with the other German *Hausfrauen,* housewives. And just like we'd done in Montreal, the three of us spent many weekends exploring our new surroundings. Elk Island Park just outside of Edmonton was everyone's favorite spot. Its lake was ice cold, but for some reason, I really enjoyed swimming in it. Mother always packed a delicious picnic that we all enjoyed.

At first, since I wasn't going to school yet and hadn't made any new friends, I spent my time walking around the nearby parks, checking out my new neighborhood church or mostly just staying cooped up in my room reading all the comic books I'd managed to accumulate.

Another thing I did later on that summer was take up tennis at the YMCA. One evening, when my parents were attending a dance there, my mother noticed an announcement about instructions. So, as it was her style to appear classy, she bought me an adorable outfit, the appropriate shoes and a brand new racket. Then, she signed me up for lessons on the facility's clay courts.

But as the summer wore on, Mother's physical and mental abuse became almost too much for me, and I couldn't wait for fall to arrive so I could get back to what I love: learning. As it turned out, I was able to adjust to my new school much more smoothly than I had in Montreal. When the time came for me to register, St. Michael's tested me and made an exception so that I could enter 7th grade, although I hadn't quite finished the 6th in Montreal because of our move.

But right after the term began, I quickly realized that I had already studied most of the subjects I was taking. When I told my parents what was happening, we all went to the principal to talk about the situation. After a teacher consultation, it was decided to let me move on to the 8th grade on a trial basis.

This worked out great for me because I loved my home room teacher, Mr. Kelly, and did quite well in all my classes. I couldn't have been prouder to bring my first report card home, not only because of the good grades it showed, but also because of the comment he wrote. "Bettina is an asset to our class."

But academics weren't the only things I liked. St. Michael's was a coed school, so I got to have my first real contact with b-o-y-s. The very first day of school, I noticed a cute, blue-eyed, blond-haired boy named Michael and immediately developed a serious crush on him. Sad to say, it went unrequited, but I still had fun imagining what being his girlfriend might be like, and at the very least knowing I would see him each day at school gave me something to look forward to.

And I made one good friend. Her name was Irene. She lived between my house and school, so almost every day I ran into her on my way there. Soon, we were walking to and from school together. Some afternoons I even stopped by her house on my way home, either to do homework or just spend the late afternoon talking in her room.

The only part of school I didn't really care for was gym class, because I was forced to play basketball, a game I'd never heard of. Needless to say, I wasn't very good at it. Because of that, and probably because I was cross-eyed and foreign, I was always picked last by the team choosers.

Since my father was making a good salary, it took him less than a year to save up enough money for a down payment on a little house for us on 72nd Street near Edmonton's Exhibition Grounds.

So, one more time, my mother informed me we were moving. And once more, I was expected to roll with the punches, to understand why I was being uprooted and to accept the situation like an adult. No one ever seemed to consider what all this moving around was doing to me.

Becoming homeowners and being able to furnish their new two-story purchase nicely was a great source of pride for my parents. It reaffirmed for them that they had made the right decision to immigrate to a land where things were so much easier and where it was so much easier to succeed.

When fall arrived, it was time for me to start high school, so I enrolled in the 9th grade at St. Joseph's, just a short bus ride from my house. I was proud that I had skipped a couple grades previously, and my goal was to graduate by the time I was seventeen. Therefore, I planned to keep my head firmly focused on my books.

Around that same time, Mother took a part time job as a housekeeper at the MacDonald Hotel. Because she wanted me to concentrate on my schoolwork, she didn't give me much responsibility for household chores or meal preparation. The only thing I remember having to do was make my bed. I suppose I'd be an even better cook today if I'd had some lessons back then, but as a typical teenager I was glad that not much was expected of me in that department.

The first week of school I met Ursula, with whom I'm still good friends to this day. She, too, was an immigrant daughter of a family that had lost everything to the Russians as they marched through Czechoslovakia. Though she also spoke German, we decided to converse in English because both of us wanted to keep working on our speaking skills. We soon became best friends.

On weekends, Ursula and I boarded buses and rode around Edmonton. We strolled along side the Saskatchewan River and through its lovely parks, often stopping to take pictures or to rest on a bench near the Capitol building. We also took our first jobs working part time for a banquet caterer at the same hotel where Mutter was employed. I didn't earn very much money, but since it was all mine, I spent it on as many up-to-the-minute fashions as I could afford and took great pride in wearing them.

Since my parents still did very little but rage at each other when my father was home, I found as many excuses as

I could to spend time at Ursula's house. Mr. and Mrs. Andres welcomed me into their home, and I relished being in their peaceful presence. I especially loved it when Ursula's mom let us help her bake cakes and cookies because watching her brought back wonderful memories of the hours I used to spend with Oma.

Sometimes I just sat and listened as my friend practiced the classical piano pieces she was learning. I was dumbfounded when Mother agreed to allow me to study music too. She would have preferred piano, but I convinced her to let me study my favorite instrument, the accordion. That very week, Mutter went out and bought a shiny, second hand accordion and enrolled me in a little music school near our home.

I was grateful to have Ursula as my friend for another reason as well. She gave me someone to lean on when adults and kids alike taunted us for being "a DP" — displaced person. All their teasing heightened Ursula's and my teenage identity crises. We were tired of sticking out like sore thumbs. We decided our foreign accents had to go. So, almost every Saturday, we showed up at the Paramount or the Odeon theaters to catch whatever double feature was being shown. It didn't matter if it was a Western, a comedy or an action-adventure picture, we knew we would be exposed to lots and lots of 'Hollywood English', both proper and slang.

Ursula wasn't my only friend. Lucky for us, the Kraus family lived right down the street from our new house. My parents really liked Mr. and Mrs. Kraus, and I got along great with their 11 year old daughter Marianne, so we all spent a lot of time together.

In fact, we became like an extended family, preparing and sharing holiday dinners and even taking the occasional overnight trip to Banff in the amazing Alberta Rockies. We'd check in to an inexpensive motel in the heart of town, then spend the day hiking the shores of Lake Louise. Or we'd pay to get into the grounds of the beautiful lakeside hotel that looked just like a fairy tale castle and then spend hours swimming in the healing waters of its spa.

We still had to economize somewhat, but now that we were so much better off materially, Mother would send monthly care packages to a few relatives and friends still struggling back in Germany. She'd shop for and carefully pack an assortment of edible goodies and personal care items; then we'd take the boxes to the post office and send them on the way with great care to those still coping back home.

When Mother wrote letters home, she filled them with stories about our new, improved life and how much she loved it. She never shared anything about missing anyone, though I'd overheard her and my father discussing their homesickness many times. In addition, when she proofread my carefully composed letters to Tante Lisbeth and Ilse, she would make me delete anything I said about missing anyone in the old country. My mother insisted that only positive thoughts about our new life make their way back to Germany.

All this time, unbeknownst to my dad, Mother's so-called "discipline" of me continued. The only change was that the frequency of beatings she rendered with her brutal wooden spoon went from several times a week to once a week. I never knew when it was coming. She'd just blow her stack for whatever reason, and the next thing I knew I'd be getting struck with her weapon of choice. Never where it would show, she'd always aim for my bottom with blows that may have varied in number but were always delivered with intensity and strength. Only once did she slip up, leaving welts on my right arm and cheek, but no one seemed to notice, not even my father.

One autumn day when I was in the 10th grade, my mother and I really got into it. She was yelling at me about one of my clothing purchases when I defiantly screamed, "You're so old fashioned!" stormed away and headed to my room upstairs. I was half way up the steps when she caught up with me wielding that evil spoon of hers.

I whirled around and fearlessly took hold of it, proclaiming, "I'm fourteen now and I don't want you to hit me anymore! I'm as big as you are, and I could hit you back. And besides, you're not always right about everything. I've got just as good taste in clothes as you, if not better, and you should let me pick out my own."

That was the last beating I received at the hands of my mother. Unfortunately, her verbal abuse continued. Mutter's obedient little girl had turned into a defiant teenager right before her very eyes.

It was around that time, too, that my parents relented and agreed to let me have the surgery I needed to correct my crossed eyes, the cause of so much torment for as long as I can remember. With my new look, my blossoming body, my 'kiss curl' and bouncy ponytail and my crinolined skirts and bobby sox, I was finally pleased with my appearance.

Each day we lived in our new country, our affinity for it grew, and it became clear we were never going to return to Germany. After a few years though, my father was forced to look for another job. Through his union pals, he learned about a well paying one on the DEW (Distant Early Warning) Line. So in 1955, off he went up to Canada's Northwest Territories, leaving my mother and me alone in Edmonton. *Mutter* still had enough power over me to demand I keep secrets regarding her comings and goings. For as long as I could remember, she subjected me to family secrets, especially ones about her activities. In my young mind, it did not seem right.

71

My confidant status was put to the test when, after six months, my father returned and started in almost at once grilling me about what mother had been up to while he'd been away. I said that I didn't know what he was talking about and immediately felt like a traitor. This feeling stuck with me until just a few years ago when I was finally able to explain to him how she dominated me.

Yet, my silence back then did not keep them from arguing. As a matter of fact, as they argued more than ever, especially about how she had behaved, I listened helplessly. Not only was she in hot water with my father, but my mother's questionable behavior had caused friction between her and the few friends my parents had made in Edmonton. She said she was just tired of them, but the truth of it was that she had managed to quickly wear out her welcome with the other German *emigres.* She found fault with everything and what everyone else did, blaming them for events that she had actually instigated. In this specific case, she claimed, "Our family wouldn't be in such a bind had my 'so-called friend' just kept quiet. Besides that, she was with me when I went out." And, once again, instead of staying and resolving conflicts, my mother convinced my father that it would be best to pick up and leave.

One day, about fifteen minutes after I'd gotten home from school, Mutter came up to my room, sat down on my bed and said, "Your father has been offered a job as a welder at a paper mill on Vancouver Island, so we'll be moving in a couple of weeks. You'll love it, Bettina. I've heard it's so beautiful there."

Once more, she wasn't asking me — she was telling me that I must now uproot myself right in the middle of 11th grade, leave my few friends and go to wherever she thought the grass was greener for her. The only difference about this

72

move was that now that we were more prosperous, an Allied Van Lines truck came to take all our belongings to our next destination — Port Alberni on Vancouver Island. Mother was right about one thing though, it was quite beautiful there.

It was obvious from my first week in the new school that the curriculum being taught was completely different, and if I was forced to continue at Port Alberni, I knew I would fail 11th grade. What upset me most was that I would not be able to graduate when I'd planned. Every day, when I'd get home from school, I'd be so upset that my folks didn't know what to do with me. Finally, after many heart-to-heart talks about the problem I was having, they agreed to let me move back to Edmonton.

My father made arrangements to pay room and board to the Andres' so that I could live in their home and reenter the 11th grade at St. Joseph's. Even though I had to play catch-up to make up for the classes I missed while I was away, I was glad to be back at my old school.

Living with the Andres' was a different story. I crammed into Ursula's tiny basement bedroom with only a few of my things, but I still felt I was imposing upon her. Then there was the calm of their household. It was such a contrast to what I was used to that I felt dreadfully out of place. I missed my own home and family, however dysfunctional they might have been.

One night, while I was concentrating on my homework, Ursula interrupted my train of thought. Since she was a grade behind me in school, I felt she simply didn't understand the pressure I was under to get caught up. Before I realized what I was doing, I began to act just like my mother, lashing out at her verbally and even going so far as to throw a hand mirror which struck her on her cheek. Immediately she screamed and began to cry.

When Mr. Andres heard all the commotion, he rushed downstairs to see what was going on. The moment he saw the scratch I had put on his precious daughter's face, he called me aside and told me in no uncertain terms that he didn't allow such outbursts under his roof. I apologized to both him and Ursula and promised I wouldn't let it happen again. From then on, I stuck to my studies and before I knew it, I had finished 11th grade and was ready to rejoin my parents.

But, while I was away, my mother had become dissatisfied with living in such a small island town and convinced my father that a move to Vancouver proper was a better idea. By the time I got back to British Columbia, good grades in hand, my father had already begun his new job there, and they had moved into a new house.

When I got off the Viscount plane from Edmonton, they both met me at the airport. They couldn't wait to take me on a tour of Vancouver and to show me my new home.

And they were right to be enthusiastic. I did like the city, our neighborhood, our house, and especially my room where I could unpack and arrange it myself. And, I liked the fact that the whole summer lay ahead for me to spend in beautiful Stanley Park, playing as much tennis as I wanted or just wandering its huge expanse.

As the end of summer approached, I went over to Gladstone High to register for 12th grade, my last year. Once again, I was an outsider in a school full of strangers.

But what was most difficult for me to deal with was the prejudice that my home room/history teacher, Mr. Church, harbored against me. Very early on in the semester, when the subject of WWII came up in class, his point of view became clear. Since I had chosen to sit in the front row, I couldn't help but notice when my teacher sent hateful glares in my direction. It made me feel like a scapegoat, like I was to blame for all the atrocities that were committed in Germany both before I was born and while I was just growing up. His dislike for me was definitely reflected in the way he graded my classwork. No matter how much time I spent on my papers or how well I did on his exams, he never gave me above a C+.His letter grades were always accompanied by hurtful, critical remarks. It wasn't bad enough that the more I learned about that time in my homeland's history, the more guilt I held inside.

I also had to deal with the fact that because of Mr. Church, my overall GPA would slide below 3.9 and that such a decline would affect my ability to complete my required courses successfully. Since Canada had very strict graduation standards and required a certain average in order to be admitted into university, I worried that this one teacher would get in the way of my reaching my goal to become a teacher myself.

Another drawback for me was that my father wouldn't allow me to go on dates. My social life was nil except for the huge crush I had on a crew-cut boy named Ken. He was in several of my classes but managed to ignore me all year long.

At year's end, my father did consent to let the prom committee match me up with another unattached nerd so I could have an escort to our senior prom. Mother and I actually had fun shopping for my pretty light blue dress, and we even found some earrings that matched perfectly. When the big evening arrived, I felt pretty as a picture, especially when my date presented me with a lovely little fresh rose corsage to pin to my dress. Off we went to the school gym where a deejay played all the popular tunes, and we danced the night away. The big thrill for me was when they called for a Ladies' Choice, and I somehow got up the courage to ask cute Ken to dance with me. I was amazed that he accepted, but I still managed to get lost in his arms for the three minutes our slow dance lasted. All in all, it was a lovely evening.

There were just a few weeks left in my final semester when my mother flew to the States to visit her cousin Nelly, or Lee as we called her, in San Diego. About a week after she got back, she and father broke the news that we were moving to the United States. After that bombshell, they recited their usual list of reasons why I was going to love it, — "America is so beautiful, Bettina. Everyone there loves Germans." It was all set.

All set for everyone but me. Once again I'd be leaving the familiar for the unfamiliar. Thank goodness that by this time my folks had learned their lesson about dragging me out of school at the wrong time. At least this time they'd waited until the end of my school year to pick up and leave, sparing me the misery of transferring before graduation.

After I'd thought about our pending move for a few days, I found myself actually looking forward to seeing and doing some of the great things I'd read and heard about the USA. And, I was especially looking forward to meeting American boys!

So, while I was busy studying for my final exams (hoping that I would do well enough to earn a GPA that would enable me to matriculate), my parents were preparing for yet another big move.

Before we left Vancouver, my folks sat me down again for one more announcement. This one was a real shocker — my mother was pregnant!

All these years, more times than I could count, I'd implored, "Why can't I have a brother or sister?" So, my first thought was, "Why now? I've been a lonely only child for seventeen years! Why not before?" But the more they talked, the more I got caught up in their excitement and the idea of finally having a sibling. So all I said was, "Well, you've already had a little girl, so I hope this one is a boy because I wouldn't mind having a little brother."

That night, in my room, I couldn't help but remember several times when my mother had been pregnant and had chosen not to keep the baby. I couldn't help but play back all the times she'd said to me, "I hope you'll be smart and never get married. You're just as well off all by yourself. You can get married when you're much older, if you want to, and not have many kids, if any. People who have a lot of children stay poor, and besides that, they're a lot of work."

I thought too, about the countless times in my young life Mutter had threatened to abandon me, "I'm going to leave you and your father and go to the farthest corner in the world where no one can find me, and I'll never have to see you again."

As I drifted off to a fretful sleep, I could only hope that she would see this one through even though it meant she would be tied down for another long period in her life. And I prayed that she would not subject my little brother or sister to the same kind of childhood I had.

Our 1949 Ford used to cross Canada

Teenager in Edmonton

Friends in Edmonton – Bettina (left) Ursula (right)

1954 - First House ever in Edmonton

Mother and her new, modern kitchen

Chapter 6

Move to USA

Almost seven years from the day we left Germany, I graduated from high school. The week after that, with only a few suitcases in hand (since my parents had once again sold or given away almost all our belongings), we said goodbye to Canada, the country that had been so good to us, and boarded the train that would take us all the way down the west coast from Vancouver, Canada to San Diego, USA.

As soon as we were underway, my life's turmoil seemed to dwindle as the glorious scenery drew me in. Each time I lowered my window to listen to the Pacific as it pounded the rocky shores, I felt better and better about my fate. By the time the palms of Southern California came into view, I was pretty sure I was coming to paradise!

Our family's adjustment to San Diego was much easier than the last time we'd moved to a new country. For starters, all of us were now much more fluent in English. For another, my parents had been able to save enough money for a better 'new beginning' this time. And, most of all, we were delighted to finally reunite with another member of our family.

Mother's cousin Lee had been living with her college professor husband, Art, in San Diego for years. So, after greeting us with a flurry of delighted hugs, the two of them couldn't wait to show us around their town. This happy couple had met when he'd come to Germany to work for Coca Cola. After a whirlwind courtship, they had gotten married and, soon thereafter, left for the States where they have been living ever since. Art and Lee insisted on chauffeuring us in

San Diego, so the first two months were great for me. They introduced us to much of what the city had to offer — an amazing Zoo, Coronado Point and several stunning beaches. As much as I loved *looking* at the ocean's majesty at first, I couldn't wait to get *into* that cool, clear water.

But it wasn't all sightseeing. Very soon after we arrived, Art and Lee introduced my father to his new employer and he began a new job. Our San Diego "angels" also helped us move right into a spacious two-bedroom furnished apartment on Iroquois Street in the Clairemont neighborhood. Not only did I enjoy all the room we now had, I was pleased to see that our building was right across the street from a place called the Clairemont Bowl.

As the summer drew to an end, one thing kept nagging at me. My parents and I had not yet discussed what university I would attend in the fall. So one evening at supper, filled with anxiety, I reluctantly brought up the subject. "I've been wondering why we haven't decided which college I should go to," I said. "I've been looking around, and I think I've found one that's not too far away and I can get to and from by bus. That's okay with me."

I sat there waiting for their response, but the only thing my father and mother did was look sheepishly at each other. After a long moment of this, they turned their gazes on me and my mother said, "We know you've been waiting patiently to talk about this, Bettina, but we have to tell you something. With all the expenses we're having to plan for with the baby, we can't really afford to send you to college."

What?! I had been so sure that the plans for my continued education were concrete. As I took in this devastating news, I saw them crumble right then and there. I studied my parents' faces, realized they were serious about their decision, and knew any argument of mine would only fall on deaf ears. There was no choice but accept the fact that an un-planned event had, at the last minute, scuttled my long held dream to become a teacher.

Mother went on, "We hope you understand, Bettina. Because of the baby, we're going to have to buy a house. Those expenses along with your education would be much too much for us to handle financially."

I was so deep in thought that I barely heard the alternate plan she was putting forth, "We'll send you to a business college so you can find a nice office job. You'll like that, too."

And then my father piped in, "Besides, you'll probably be getting married in a few years anyway. So, what's the point of your going to college anyway?"

Still in disbelief, I screamed, "All this time you both liked the idea of my becoming a teacher! I don't *want* to be an office worker!" I jumped up from the table and started to sob violently as I ran into my room. Having been dismissed and short changed yet again, I stayed there crying for days. Then, I stuffed this new disappointment deep inside along with all my other long buried hurts and went about preparing for "Plan B."

About a week after that life altering crisis, I began attending Kelsey-Jenney Business College located in the heart of downtown San Diego. After completing a three month course to improve my office skills, I had no trouble finding a position as a receptionist and bookkeeper at Liberty Loan in the Clairemont Shopping Center directly across the street from our apartment.

Throughout her pregnancy, my mother had seemed more mellow and subdued than her norm. But three weeks after I started my new job, I got a frantic phone call from her.

"Bettina, you have to come home right away! My water broke! I need you to take me right to the hospital. Now! First, call us a taxi and then get right over here!"

Since I'd already informed my new boss about our situation, all I had to do was tell him, "My mother's in labor so I'm leaving." By the time I got back over to our building, Mother was already outside tightly clutching her little suitcase, waiting for me and the cab. It finally arrived and off the two of us went to Sharp Memorial Hospital. Thirty minutes later my father joined me in the maternity ward waiting room. There we sat for what seemed like forever until we were startled by my mother's voice booming over the loudspeaker, "Our Brencher baby is here! It's a boy!"

From the very first moment I set eyes on Baby Bill, all my resentment was set aside, and I was thrilled that my wish for a little brother, no matter how delayed, had finally come true.

When Mother and the baby got home from the hospital, I offered to pitch right in to help, except I refused to change diapers. I thought that Mother should be the one to take care of that unpleasant task.

When Bill was awake, I loved cooing and talking baby talk with him just to see his adorable reactions. And sometimes, when he was tucked into his crib, I would sit alongside it and watch my cute and fragile little brother sleep his blissful sleep.

But, as much as I loved Little Bill, he couldn't keep my interest for long. I was now much more interested in finding other objects of love — boys. Since I hadn't been allowed to date all through high school, I was ready to make up for lost time.

There I was, a pretty young working girl, still living under one small roof with my pre-occupied parents and a crying, new infant. As long as I had to be patient and put up with all that, I figured I could spend some of my hard earned money on fabulous clothes and begin going out with a vengeance.

Luckily, I had met my new friend Liz at Business School to help me. Since she was one year older and had been allowed to date while in high school, she already knew the ropes and was more than willing to show them to me. Liz drove a fabulous '58 pink and white 2-door Mercury coupe, a high school graduation gift from her mother. The two of us would get in that snazzy car to cruise all the local beaches and Jack-in-the-Box drive-ins, flirting with as many cool guys as we could. After befriending some of the good looking ones, Liz and I double-dated to Disneyland or to the beaches so I could get the hang of the dating game under her watchful eye. Being around so many young, gorgeous American men was like a dream come true for me.

One afternoon, soon after I had begun tagging along with Liz, she and I went shopping for something great to wear the following weekend. With both of us crowded in a tiny dressing room, I pulled my top off to try on a blouse. When she got a good look at my face, I heard her sort of gasp and say, "Wow! You look great without glasses! Do you have to wear those things all the time? I think the hot guys would pay more attention to you if you didn't." From that time on, whenever I went out, my glasses came off. So what if I couldn't see anything or anyone up close.

One of the most convenient destinations for our cruise-a-thons was right next door to my apartment building. The Stardust Room in the Clairemont Bowl rocked every single weekend . Don't ask me how Liz and I even got into the Bowl's bar (where alcohol was served) without our IDs being checked, but we did it. Sometimes we made it out onto the dance floor ourselves, not only to rock the bee bop, but to twist the summer nights away dancing to Chubby Checker's infectious beat.

It was right around then that I became acquainted with a young man with whom I'm still good friends. Liz and I would often go out to the nearby Naval Air Base for weekend dances. It was at one of these parties that we met Tom Monroe, a young petty officer. Tom and Liz really hit it off and dated for a few months. But even after they stopped dating, he and I stayed in touch, a situation I'd be very grateful for just a few years down the road.

Let me tell you, my father wasn't at all pleased with these new activities of mine. "I don't want to meet any of these guys unless you're going to marry 'em!" Occasionally, the two of them would slack up a bit and become curious about one of my boyfriends. When that happened, I'd bring him home for an introduction. But, for the most part, I was behaving just like my mother had done throughout her life — looking for love anywhere but where I lived.

About eight months after Bill was born, my parents bought a two bedroom, one bath house. To me, the new place still seemed uncomfortably small, but since I wanted to save money, I decided it would be a good idea if I moved into it with them.

And it was a good idea — until one evening when I was relaxing in the bathtub after a particularly frustrating day. My little brother was in the midst of his terrible twos, so he thought nothing of barging in on me and innocently exclaiming, "Tina, l wanna play."

At that moment, feeling like my privacy was invaded, I just lost it, yelling at the top of my lungs for him to get out.

93

My mother heard the commotion and came running. When she saw Bill crying, she instantly turned on me and said, "You have no right to tell him what to do! That's my job, not yours."

In the middle of that hot tempered moment, it became clear to me that it didn't matter how unfair *I* thought it was that he wasn't being as firmly disciplined as I had been. The only thing that mattered was her opinion. The end result? That very night I packed my things and left my parents' house for good.

There I was on my own at twenty. Well, almost. I moved in with Anne Ebert, my friend from the Savings and Loan Association, and for about a year, I shared her adorable one bedroom apartment near one of San Diego's great beaches. Both she and my other friend Liz helped make my adjustment to living away from home a lot easier for me.

After my dramatic exit, my mother and I didn't speak for six months. When I couldn't take our separation any longer, I finally broke the ice by writing her and asking if we could at least be civil. A few days later, she called me to acknowledge my letter, but instead of making up, all she did was moan that I had broken her heart. She told me she'd taken it for granted that I would follow the old German tradition of living under her roof until I got married, and that I had disappointed her by moving out.

Despite its negativity, that short conversation cracked the door open, and from then on, we occasionally spoke, but only when necessary and only superficially. I shared very little of my new lifestyle with her.

Around this time, Liz and I started to go out with two cute guys we met right on Mission Beach. Liz' romance soon fizzled, but John and I kept dating for almost two more years. He was a highway engineer and was about five years older, but that didn't seem to matter. I just loved hanging out with him for hours while he worked on his white (sported with two wide black stripes in the center from front to back) Corvette. We would drink beer and listen to light jazz coming from the radio sitting on his garage floor. I also loved all the snuggling we did whenever we had the chance.

Having a "car freak" for a boyfriend came in quite handy when I turned 21 and was old enough to sign papers for a loan. John helped me pick out — you guessed it — a '57 bronze 'Vette with both a soft and hard top. Then he helped me spruce up the interior until it was just the way I wanted it with a padded dashboard and a customized tano cover.

Yes, my life seemed perfect. I was working and living in Pacific Beach, I had all the independence I could want, I had a new car, and I was with John.

But my paradise was soon lost. One January morning in 1962, after not hearing from him or being able to reach him for several days, I went over to John's apartment. Since everything seemed fine just the weekend before when we'd attended a Corvette rally, I wasn't too concerned. I was dead wrong! I found his place completely emptied out — with no sign that he had ever lived there! When I called John's office at the California Department of Highways, all the secretary would say was that he had transferred but didn't know where.

Once again in my young life, I sort of went into shock. I think I felt so desperate because I had no inkling *at all* that he was going to leave. For days after his vanishing act, I searched everywhere I could think to look, but to no avail.

I was utterly crushed that he had chosen to disappear without saying one word to me. When I thought about it, the only justification I could come up with was that he didn't think I fit into his life anymore and he was too afraid to tell me. The story I told myself was he probably moved back to San Francisco where he had family — and whoever else.

Like my mother merely threatened to do so many times, John had actually gone ahead deserted me. Even after the initial shock wore off, I stayed bewildered and in deep pain for months.

I was still reeling from John's abandonment when I was handed some more bad news. One evening at supper, after Anne and I had been roommates for close to a year, I noticed that she seemed very preoccupied. When I asked her what was up, she went into a long explanation about how good it had been sharing an apartment with me but that now she wanted her boyfriend Jim to move in with her.

The same week I found out I would have to move, my friend Liz told me she would be moving out of state. All this time, she'd been living with and caring for her elderly mother who wanted to return to Florida.

Liz told me, "Bettina, I'd hoped we could be friends forever, but I have no choice but to go with her."

Once again, I felt like I'd been socked in the stomach, but this time, at least, it wasn't as final since Liz and I vowed to stay in touch. Indeed, we have remained good friends all these years.

With Anne and Liz' help, it didn't take long to find a cute furnished studio apartment that I could afford by myself. Not only was it close to work, but it also had a lovely view of Mission Bay.

Just a month after I'd settled in, my folks told me they were moving to New York City! I knew my father had been having trouble finding steady work, but I couldn't believe my mother had convinced him that a better life awaited them there. I guess he finally faced the reality that the construction boom in San Diego had ended and caved into her fantasies once again.

I was kind of surprised when they asked if I wanted to go with them. I told them, however, that I loved California and didn't want to leave. So off went my family across the country — without me.

Even though I was glad I'd stayed behind, I still felt desperately lonely without my friend Liz and my family nearby. What did I do to fill the void? I went out searching for another boyfriend. It didn't take long.

One night, at a nearby beach bar, I met Bill and it was "lust at first sight." I couldn't resist his handsome face, red hair and sweet, polite manner. It must have been the same for him because, over the next two months, we saw each other a lot, although we both knew we weren't that serious about each other.

Then the worst possible thing happened. Just like my mother had done twenty years earlier, I discovered I was pregnant! When I could no longer deny the reality, I called Bill and asked him to come over as soon as possible. I knew I had to tell him, even if I had no clue as to what I wanted to do about it. An hour later he showed up, and I gave him the bad news.

Just like me, he was stunned. But, unlike me, Bill knew exactly how he felt about it. He apologized and said he couldn't imagine getting married or having a child at that point in his life. Since the thought of settling down scared me too, and since I knew I didn't love him, I had to agree with him that we shouldn't see it through. So it was goodbye to the once sweet Bill and hello to utter panic.

I could see no other solution to my nightmare but to turn to my parents. By this time, they'd given up on New York and had resettled in Las Vegas. So I gave my notice at

97

work and, in my numbed-out state, moved away from my once carefree life in beautiful San Diego to join my parents in the glitter city.

Shortly after I got there, the decision was made. There was only one way out of my darkness: an abortion. My 'helpful' parents then told me that they knew a way out but they made me promise not to ever, *ever* tell anyone about it.

Obedient child that I was, for over twenty years I kept the fact that I had ever been pregnant a secret. Then, at the age of 45, for the first time, I confessed it outside of the church to my trusted friend Peggy. Instead of turning against me, she was altogether compassionate and told me how proud she was of me for carrying that awful cross alone for so long. But, even with support from her and my therapists over the ensuing years, all I could ever manage to say was that there was a miscarriage, not an abortion. I still couldn't bring myself to reveal the episode's traumatic details until the summer of 2000.

That's when I attended a Creative Writing Workshop at The Omega Institute in upstate New York. On my second day there, the workshop leader gave us an assignment to write about a horrific event in our lives. Then he mentioned that its recall could come more easily if we told the story in the third person rather than the first. Thus, I was given the key to unlock my nightmare of guilt. This is what I wrote:

In the middle of the night, an ambulance came to rush a young woman, twenty-two years of age, to the hospital. Her mother had called a doctor, afraid for her daughter's life. She told him, "My daughter has been bleeding for three days. We don't know what's wrong with her!" Of course her mother knew, but she was in fear of the law and of the Church. Besides, she had to keep the family secret. The young woman was placed in a dark maternity ward and left to fend for herself. Around her, other beds were occupied but she felt so very alone. The pain hurt her so much. "What's going on with me?" she moaned. "You're having labor pains because you're having a baby," a woman's voice spoke from somewhere in the dark room. "Nooooo!" the young woman screamed and then she begged, "Jesus, please help me! Help me!" But the pain was unrelenting. Finally, after what seemed like an eternity, with one last contraction, the confused girl pushed the dead fetus out and was overcome with tremendous relief. It was then that a nurse finally came to her bedside to assure her the worst was over.

The next day, after cleaning her insides out, the doctor reassured her that she would be okay. "You are young and you still have a good long life ahead of you. You can make a new start." The young girl wasn't so sure.

Looking back, I can see that the optimistic doctor meant well, but at the time, I couldn't bring myself to believe a word he said. For months, I lived alone in such fear, shame and guilt that I finally forced myself to do what I had been taught all along by my Catholic Church. I went to confession, and the priest gave me absolution for a mortal sin. God may have been merciful, but I had no mercy of my own.

I could only see myself as an emotional wreck at twenty-two, with no instructions in the art of how to love myself or others. Yet, all along I had been so sure I could "do life" better than my parents had! Despite my set back, I did somehow manage to pull myself together.

Perhaps my German perseverance is what got me through the ordeal. Yet, I once again buried my pain and fear deep inside, put on a happy mask and blindly stumbled on. After taking a path of spiritual growth, I now know that God takes care of me all the time.

1958 San Diego awaiting arrival of Baby Bill

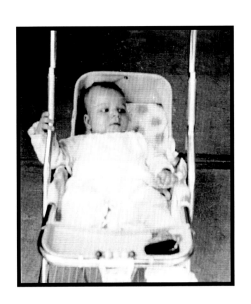

Baby Bill

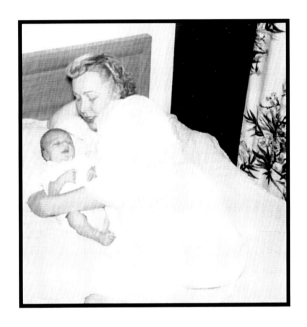

Mother with Brother Bill

Proud Daddy

**Friends, Liz (left), Bettina (right)
at a San Diego Beach**

Loving my '57 Corvette

Chapter 7

The Foggy Years

Only three weeks after the terrible event, I began my job as a teller at Nevada Savings and Loan Association. Until I could save up enough money to move into another place, I lived with my family in their small apartment.

During the week, I was fortunate to be busy and glad to have the opportunity to make new friends at the S & L. Weekends, I put the Corvette top down and attempted to escape my feelings by tooling around to places of interest like Hoover Dam and Mt. Charleston. Many nights I cruised the Vegas Strip or Casino Center, trying my luck at a few slot machines, fantasizing that I could turn my self-imposed $20 limit into something more.

I wasn't earning much but used most of my hard earned money to improve my appearance. One of the first things I did was find a convenient beauty salon where I could get my hair and nails done. That's where I met Joanie, my manicurist. In typical beauty shop tradition, it didn't take long for me to share with her that I was staying with my parents while looking for an apartment.

To my complete surprise, she said, "Hey, I'm ready to move too, because my two roommates are just a little too wild for me. Looks like we were meant to meet. What do you think about the two of us looking for a place?"

Since I liked Joanie from the first moment I sat down at her table, I jumped at her suggestion. Within a couple of weeks, we'd moved to Charleston Heights at the outskirts of town and into a brand new building with a pool.

It was ideal. Our furnished two bedroom apartment

gave the two of us plenty of personal space. And, not only was I able to leave my parents but my roommate became my lifelong friend. My life had taken a turn for the better.

Just before Joanie and I moved to Charleston Heights, I began dating a real estate broker I'd met at the S & L. His name was Ray, and since my transfer into the Escrow Department, I'd been assigned to work with him. One day after Ray dropped off a new contract for me to process, he surprised me by saying, "If you're not attached, I'd sure like to take you out to dinner." Even though he didn't fit the picture of a dreamboat, I liked his air of confidence, so I accepted.

That afternoon, I hurried home from work, took a quick bath and put on my stylish red Jackie Kennedy suit with its smart fur collar. When Ray picked me up at 6:30, the first thing he did before he opened the door of his sleek, white '61 Cadillac, was compliment me on how great I looked. I soaked up his admiration like a thirsty person in the desert. I felt even more special when I discovered he'd chosen one of Vegas' most popular places to dine that evening.

As we entered the restaurant, Ray guided me into its bar, explaining that he always liked to have a cocktail before dinner. This was all new to me, so when the waitress asked me what I'd like to drink, I shrugged my shoulders and turned to Ray.

With certainty, he interjected, "Bring her a martini with a twist, and I'll have the same." Martini? Sounded quite exotic to me because, up to that point in my life, I'd only had a few beers. Filled with curiosity, I was more than willing to go along. With our drinks in hand, we raised them and toasted to a great first date. Then I took a first cautious sip of the deceptively clear cocktail.

"Wow, that's bitter!" I exclaimed.

"Just wait a little bit," Ray advised. So I took another sip and then another, both of which went down like a bitter medicine. But, just as he had promised, within moments, a fuzzy warmth overcame me and I began to feel more relaxed than I ever remembered feeling.

Before I could finish my now treasured drink, we were escorted to our table. When the waiter took our order, Ray selected a bottle of red wine to accompany our steak and lobster. I was amazed how each smooth sip of it made me feel better and better! Little did I know that I had just discovered the tool that would let me pretend that my life's traumas had never happened. That evening of social drinking was the beginning of my alcohol abuse. My 'foggy years' had begun.

It was also the beginning of my turbulent three year relationship with Ray. Looking back on it now, I can see that Ray was also drowning his sorrows. Turns out he had recently divorced and was sending money to his ex-wife and their three children whom he rarely got to see.

We became social butterflies, drinking our nights away and catching Wayne Newton or whoever was appearing in the Glitter City's many casino lounges. While he wined and dined and made successful deals with local builders, I was his trophy gal, perfectly content to sit by his side and sip the delicious martinis he kept ordering and paying for!

I guess it was inevitable that all our drinking would cause trouble. Within a year, we began having terrible arguments about what I perceived to be his incessant flirting and subsequent inattention to me.

My insecurity was so out of control that one night I even accused my completely innocent roommate of seducing him! But, the next morning, I'd sobered up enough to listen while Joanie told me what had actually happened. Evidently, Ray had shown up drunk at our front door. Since she didn't want him to stick around, she had more or less shoved him all the way outside and into her car. Then, to help sober him up, she took him to get something to eat. I was even able to manage a smile when she described how he nodded off into his salad. Right after dinner, she'd driven him back to his apartment and got him inside his door safe and sound. When she was through telling me the whole story, I had no choice but to thank her for putting up with both me and my unruly boyfriend.

In the winter of 1963, that sad time after President Kennedy's assassination, Joanie started dating a man named Jim. After a short, intense courtship, they decided to get married. But her happy news meant that I was apartment hunting again!

I asked Ray to check with his builder buddies, and sure enough, one of them had a small one-bedroom apartment available in a building he owned. And by January 1964, I had settled into my new place. I liked it for many reasons, including its great view of the pool and proximity to work.

The move didn't seem to change much between Ray and me. We stayed stuck in our fight-and-make-up loop, going nowhere fast. In my naive and deluded mind, I thought getting married might be the answer. When I suggested this to Ray, he said, "I am willing to put a diamond on your finger, but I don't think I'll ever get married again." The more pressure I applied, the more Ray would push me away and for the record, I never got a ring.

Toward the end of that year, I began not hearing from him for days at a time. In a jealous frenzy, I often went searching for him in our favorite hangouts. Once or twice, I did spot him sitting with girls and guys I didn't know, but I didn't have the nerve to confront him. I just went home and cried my eyes out over his betrayal. When Ray called me the next day to try to explain away what I had witnessed the night before, he acted as if he'd not done anything wrong. Despite his protestation, I knew in my gut he was seeing other women.

One night, I followed him to an unfamiliar apartment building, parked right next to his car and waited. After several hours, I'd had enough of that so I decided to circle the block a couple of times. When I drove off, I guess Ray must have recognized the powerful sound of my Corvette's motor and realized that he couldn't leave the same way he'd come in. By the time I circled back around to the scene of the crime, I witnessed my disheveled boyfriend climbing out of another woman's back window with his jacket and tie slung over his arm. And then I watched as he furtively made his way to his car and drove off.

My thoughts were hopscotching between "How could he?" and "I've got to break up with this man!" In tears, I followed him back to his place and drove home to face another miserable night in my lonely apartment. When Ray came to my apartment after work the next day, I demanded an explanation for his activities the night before. He was shocked that I knew! It didn't take long for the exchange to heat up. Before I could stop myself, I slapped him hard. He countered with a closed fisted punch to my face and stormed out. The following morning, when I caught a glimpse of my swollen black eye in the mirror, I called work and told them I was sick and wouldn't be coming in. I spent the next few days nursing my physical wounds and my battered emotions. At some point, what was left of my pride and common sense must have kicked in because, when Ray called to check up on me, I was able to say to him, "I'm too upset to talk with you. In fact, I don't ever want to see you again!" And that was that.

Those next few weeks, I was living a "when it rains, it pours" kind of life. Just days after Ray's exit, in the dead of night, my precious Corvette was stolen from in front of my apartment! Three days later, the police called to tell me they had found my car in the desert, stripped and stranded. That's exactly how I was feeling. But a month later, I felt a little better when my insurance company handed over a $1400 check to compensate for my loss.

I'd never had so much money at one time, and I knew exactly what I was going to do with it — I was going back to Germany to see the family I'd left so many years before!

When I told my parents of my plan, all my mother said was, "Go ahead and go, but don't talk too much about us. Tell only the good things, not the bad."

Over the years, my father made my mother pay for insisting they leave Germany in the first place. One way was to put his foot down whenever she brought up the idea of going back, refusing ostensibly until they were in much better shape financially. The sad truth was that they'd been living in North America for thirteen years, but that was still to happen. And now they both expected me to keep the secret about their lack of prosperity from our relatives back home.

"If they ask you why we don't come to visit, just tell them we're raising Bill, and we're just too busy to make the trip right now. Be sure to say that we're enjoying our lives."

No way was I going to let their concerns stop me. In December of '64, I flew from Las Vegas to New York to board a Lufthansa flight to Germany. I landed in Düsseldorf, where Tante Lisbeth, Onkel Fritz and Cousin Ilse met me with hugs, tears and a big bouquet of flowers. We piled into their big Mercedes for the short drive to Mülheim. Ilse and I

119

sat in the back seat, chattering the entire time, just like we'd done when we were little girls. No one could have shut us up even if they had wanted to!

Before they had come to fetch me, Tante Lisbeth had set a beautiful table to welcome me to their home. The minute we entered their apartment, she went into the kitchen to brew a pot of coffee and slice the wonderful marble cake she had lovingly baked in my honor. While she was doing that, I joined everyone else in the living room. I chose to sit where I could have a good view of a painting I had loved since I was a little girl. It was a pastoral scene depicting some field workers and a hay wagon that was being pulled by two workhorses. To be back in that apartment, surrounded by so many familiar things, was almost more than I could bear. Between my imposing jet lag and my heightened emotions, I was a happy basket case, ready for a good long nap.

The next morning, Tante Lisbeth's quiet voice roused me out of my sound sleep. *"Bettina, aufwachen. Dein Frühstück ist vertig.* Bettina, wake up. Your breakfast is ready."* And indeed it was — a platter brimming with sliced ham and cheese, a basket filled with pumpernickel and rye breads and *Brötchen* rolls fresh from the local bakery. A selection of jam was at each place and a tiny cup holding a soft boiled egg. We all sat around the breakfast table talking, catching up on the last thirteen years of our eventful lives.

That afternoon, my family took me on a tour around the rebuilt, clustered cities of Mülheim, Oberhausen, Essen, and Düsseldorf. I was so amazed that I couldn't detect any signs of destruction of war. It seemed surreal to me as we drove through the streets where people were hustling and bustling as they would in any modern city in the world. Nothing seemed familiar until we visited the old city center of Mülheim when I spotted an old cathedral I had visited with

Tante Lisbeth. My heart enjoyed that moment of childhood memory.

Since I'd arrived, *Onkel* Fritz had let us women do all the talking. But that evening over dinner, he finally got brave enough to say, "Ja, Bettina, now that you have seen how nice it is, don't you and your parents want to come back here?"

I couldn't tell if my uncle was serious or not, but I became a bit defensive anyway. I gave him my honest reply.

"No, Onkel, I'm happy we moved to America and so are my parents. We love it there. I'm pretty sure none of us could ever think of moving back."

Onkel Fritz raised his eyebrows but, for the moment, he seemed to accept what I'd said. Thank goodness my Aunt Lisbeth interrupted, "We would love to have you here for your entire visit, *Schätzchen,* (little treasure or precious one) but your Oma Brencher and relatives on your father's side want to see you, too."

So, we phoned my only living grandparent, who told me through her tears that she'd been anxiously waiting to hear from me. She also told me to please hurry up and get over there because there were many family gatherings planned in my honor.

Around noon the next day, I said goodbye to my mother's side of the family. It wasn't so hard because I knew I'd be back in a few days. Then, my uncle took me to Oma's small apartment in nearby Oberhausen, a city famous for its coal mines, which were no longer active.

Oma Brencher greeted me with more joyful tears and, almost before I entered the threshold, led me to the big table where she'd set the lunch she'd spent all morning preparing. The two of us sat there, eating and reminiscing for a couple of hours. Being in my grandmother's home brought back even more memories of my childhood. Why, I could almost see my beloved Opa Brencher sitting on the sofa smoking his pipe! And I recalled the times we had all squeezed into this tiny place for special family occasions.

My dear Oma couldn't seem to contain herself! Just like a mother, she kept repeating how much she missed her son. Even when I reassured that her Willy was doing just fine in America, she kept telling me that she wished he had never left. Grandmother was very careful not to place blame, but it was hard for me not to feel like a scapegoat for the decisions my parents had made.

Oma and I spent the rest of the afternoon looking at hundreds of old photos. When I asked her if I could keep the ones I really liked, she was delighted to oblige. Since I was still tired from traveling, we decided to go to bed early so we'd both be fresh for the next day's events.

The following morning, our heart-to-heart talks continued over several cups of her good, strong coffee. Then, after lunch, one of my cousins picked us up and took us over to my Onkel Erich and Tante Maria's house for the big party.

That evening, my aunts, uncles and cousins arrived one by one to meet me and check me out. I felt I was some sort of celebrity when they marveled at how I'd grown up to be such a beautiful young woman. Of course, they wanted to know everything about me and my family, and I did my best to paint a good picture of our lives in Las Vegas. I even invited them to visit us so they could see for themselves.

Even though everyone was very kind, I felt like I was under a microscope. But thanks to the Schnapps and liqueurs they introduced me to, I was able to breeze through my recounting of the past thirteen years with relative ease.

After several delightful days in Oberhausen, Onkel Fritz picked me up to return me to Mülheim. I spent two more days with cousin Ilse and family, but then my all too brief and very emotional visit to Germany came to an end. At the airport, we said *Auf Wiedersehen*, and I assured them I would not wait another thirteen years to come back.

Once on the airplane, I was able to reflect on my visit. While it was somewhat stressful to answer everyone's questions, I was happy to have seen my family. The excitement of the trip far outweighed the difficulties I may have encountered. My journey had been a success!

When I got back to Las Vegas, I rested up for a few days and then began to shop for another car. It only took me a week to find a snazzy, white, 2-door '61 Chevy Impala that I fell in love with. With the money that was left over from my insurance settlement, I proudly made a small down payment because I felt secure about my job at Nevada Savings & Loan, I didn't think I'd have any problem making my payments each month.

But all too soon, my optimistic bubble burst when the Vegas building boom went bust. As our S & L began to foreclose on many of its builders' construction loans, it was forced to reduce its Escrow Department to a skeleton staff. In May of 1965, I became yet another casualty of the recession.

They say that everything depends on timing, God's good timing I say now. Because what seemed like a potential disaster soon became my golden opportunity. When I got the all important phone call from my friend Tommy Monroe that summer day, I was free to interview with his airline and to begin immediately — and thus began my 38-year flying career.

1964 – Leaving Las Vegas for Germany

1964 Reunited – Ilse (left) Bettina (right)

Part II

My Flying Career

(Please note that this part of the book was originally written while I was still flying.)

Chapter 8

Landing the "Stewardess" Job

The Interview

Back in July of 2001, just two months before the events of September 11, I was sailing through a cloudless summer sky aboard an A320 airbus, working the first day of my four day duty trip.

Susan (a fellow flight attendant whom I didn't know very well) and I had completed the lunch service, so we went back to the rear galley and settled down on the double jumpseat for a short break. This tiny space, lovingly dubbed our psychology chair, gives us safe space to get acquainted, share our thoughts, vent and support each other.

On this day, as it often did, the icebreaker subject of career longevity came up. "This is a very special trip for me," I said.

"Why's that?" Susan asked.

"Because, as of tomorrow morning , I've been flying for exactly 36 years. It boggles my mind to think I've flown over 15,000,000 miles during this time. You can't imagine all the changes I've experienced. Believe me, it's been quite a ride!"

"That's terrific, Bettina! I've got seventeen years in, and I still like it but I've gotta tell you, lately I've been getting the urge to move on to something more meaningful. I've noticed that you are still very enthusiastic and was wondering how you've been able to maintain such a good attitude for such a long time?"

"Thanks," I said.

"That's because this life's really been good to me!

And I've been thinking about that very question myself." I wanted to explain further, but just then, we were interrupted by a passenger asking for a glass of water.

As I silently went about my work, I thought about what I would have said next to Susan, "To start with, I've always loved what I was doing. And I've learned to look at all these years as a gift providing me with the perfect combination of stability and the freedom *to seek* and *find* 'smoother air' — the happiness and peace of mind all of us seem to yearn for. If Mother Earth is our school, then for me, the sky has been my classroom. "

But I had only found the contentment that Susan sensed in me after putting myself though a lot of soul-searching — many pain filled years — before I realized that the air is much calmer when I remember that I am *always* flying with God.

If the truth be told, I hadn't even considered that the time for self-exploration might be a perk when I signed up for an airline career. It appealed to me in the first place because I knew I wouldn't be stuck in a 9-to-5 rut. Well, I sure got what I asked for in that respect — schedules that were never the same from month-to-month or even from day-to-day.

But the perks don't end there. I've been able to meet people from all over the world and have formed lifelong friendships with some amazing co-workers. And, since I've been surrounded by upbeat new hires all along the way, I've managed to stay pretty young at heart. Even though I've never felt like I was getting any older, the years have just flown by because *nothing* about this job has ever been routine. And to think that an airline career was only my second choice. All through high school, my heart was set on teaching. But when my parents couldn't afford to send me to college, I decided to move on to 'Plan B'. I began to chase a career in flying, and I am grateful to this day that, back in 1965, I landed my job as a stewardess.

Forty years ago, single young ladies dreamt about a career in the air like young women (and men) today envision a career in deep space. Becoming a stewardess wasn't an easy thing to do because there were many more applicants than openings for such a desirable job. I found that out in 1961 when I applied at two airlines. To my dismay, I wasn't hired by either and had to table my primary goal.

Disappointed, I let my stewardess dream fade away and took a position as a bookkeeper at Home Federal Savings and Loan of San Diego. When I moved to Las Vegas in 1962, I became a cashier at Nevada Savings. I fit right in to that place's cheerful atmosphere, and over time, I managed to work my way up from drive-in teller to assistant escrow officer.

But since escrow work is dependent on the cycle of the real estate market, when that market collapsed after three years, my work also came to a screeching halt. In mid-May of '65, I opened my pay envelope to find a pink slip attached to my check! I was so shocked that I began to cry agonizing tears. I had observed others losing *their* jobs but *never* expected *it* to happen to *me*! Here I was, a hard working German immigrant girl, dismissed! I felt utterly disgraced! My coworkers tried to comfort me, explaining that being laid off due to downsizing was not a failure, not like being fired. Nothing they said could soothe the pain and shame I felt inside as I cleaned out my desk and forlornly walked out the door. For the next two weeks, I secluded myself in my apartment, crying almost non-stop and worrying about my future. I knew I had no choice but to make a change, but exactly what that change would be I didn't yet know.

While I wallowed in my concern over what would happen next, I had no idea that God already had a plan for me. In my time of misery, my phone rang. When I picked up the receiver, I was shocked to hear Tom Monroe's voice say,

"Hey, BB, remember me?" Did I ever! My friend Liz and I had met Tommy years before at a dance in San Diego, where he was stationed with the Navy. He dated Liz for a while and we all became such good friends that I didn't mind that he shortened my name from Bettina Brencher to BB. When he and Liz quit seeing each other, we remained buddies and stayed in touch at first. But, after I moved to Las Vegas, two years had gone by without a word from him. So, when I answered the phone, I was pleasantly surprised to hear his familiar voice.

"I'm not in the Navy anymore, BB. I've been here in Vegas for almost a year working as a mechanic at Bonanza Airlines. I would've gotten in touch with you sooner, but I've had a *real* hard time finding your phone number."

We spent twenty minutes or so catching up on what had been going on in both of our lives for the last two years. Then Tommy wondered aloud, "Am I remembering right BB? Didn't you want to become a stewardess when we both lived in San Diego?"

"What a question! Of course I did! I can't believe you remembered!" My insides stirred with curiosity.

"Yes, I did. And today, when I heard that Bonanza is still looking to fill the next stewardess class, I thought of you right away. I knew I had to do whatever it would take to get in touch with you, especially since I am friends with the Personnel Manager. I have already told him about you and since time is of the essence, I'll bring you an application and will even hand it in for you." I took him up on his offer without a moment's hesitation. And for hours after we had

133

hung up, his words kept ringing in my head: Airline Stewardess! Me, a STEWARDESS! My dream could still come true! Tommy came by that evening, handed me the paperwork and sat patiently while I filled it out.

I was thrilled when two days later Bonanza called me to set up for a personal interview. This time I was ready for them! I went into that interviewer's office armed with much more enthusiasm and confidence than I'd shown four years earlier — and with a sharper appearance to match. My being fluent in German was also a big plus for me, as it still is for any bilingual applicant today.

Although I felt pretty good about myself, my interview felt like *The Inquisition* because the personnel manager kept firing questions at me: "What would you do if you had an illness on board? How would you handle passengers if the gear collapsed on landing?"

I answered, "I want to take care of people, and I am sure with proper training I'll be able to handle these situations when they come up."

"How do you think you can contribute to our airline?"

"Well, with my love for people and my travel experiences, I'll give friendly service and understanding!" I was saying everything I could think of to sell myself. When I was asked to read the flight announcement card, I took my time and spoke clearly, aware that the piercing eyes of my interrogator were focused solely upon me.

Finally, after what seemed like hours of scrutiny, my 'inquisitor' became my 'soon-to-be employer' when he smiled at me and said, "It looks like you're hired. All I have to do is review your application with the head of your department. When that's done, we'll notify you in writing."

For ten days that sweltering summer, I anxiously checked my mailbox for the magic envelope. When it finally arrived, I tore it open on the spot and the words I had been waiting for jumped right off the page, "Congratulations! You have been accepted as a candidate to be a 'hostess' for Bonanza Airlines. Your training begins on July 19, 1965."

I rushed inside and headed for the phone! The first person I called was my recently re-discovered friend. "Tommy! Tommy!" I was so excited I could barely get the words out, "I got the job! They hired me!"

"I knew they would, BB. That's just great!"

"If it hadn't been for you, this airline dream would have never come true for me! Thank you! Thank you! Thanks a million!"

"My pleasure, girl. I'll see you after your training." He sounded genuinely happy for me. A year after I had embarked on my joyful stewardess job, Tommy announced he was marrying a stewardess who graduated in the training class after me. I congratulated him and said that I was as happy about his future life just as he'd been about my new flying career. I wasn't at all surprised that Tommy moved up our company's management ladder, and I'm glad to report that we've remained good friends to this day.

After my conversation with Tommy, I called my parents. When my mother answered, I rattled off the good news to her in German. She was *very* excited for me, *"Das ist ja wunderbar! So einen schoenen Beruf! Ich freue mich und bin sehr stolz auf Dich!* That's terrific! What a great job! I am so happy for you and very, very proud."

I telephoned a few more friends to announce that I'd been hired by Bonanza. They, too, cheered me on with comments like: "Outstanding!" "That sounds like something you'll really enjoy." " I know you'll be great at it!" Even though the times were seething with currents of war, civil rights marches and flower power; and even though that Elvis

Presley star rocked the music world around the clock, and the Beatles screamed to hold my hand— I heard none of it. My focus was only on flying— the word used by pilots and stewardesses to refer to their airline work. My anticipation was incredible! I couldn't wait to find out what this new life in the sky had in store for me.

Training

But first there was the training. It was the same back then as it is now — each airline provided its own. Bonanza's involved an intensive course that began with four weeks of Ground School where we learned first aid, emergency and service procedures. This was followed by two weeks of both group and solo hands-on training flights. After six grueling weeks of classes, homework and tests, my fellow graduates and I beamed with a sense of accomplishment as our wings were pinned to the lapels of our sparkling new uniforms.

Throughout the training, my excitement about the job only grew. After all, I was among the vanguard of women who'd been invited to become the newest participants in this relatively new industry. Before this, airlines had relied mostly on nurses (both male and female) to serve as on-board personnel to take care of any illnesses and to be present in case of disasters.

I was entering a changing and growing airline business when airline executives began to re-think that practice, deciding to put more emphasis on luxury and comfort. To fly back then was truly an event and every passenger dressed up in his Sunday best. Since most were well off— movie stars, sports figures, politicians and the like — the executives' thinking was that our own passengers are

136

important and they need more pampering. Why not hire beautiful single women to take care of these beautiful people?

This mid-50's decision was monumental: airline hostesses, not only trained in first aid and emergency procedures, but lovely and charming, soon replaced the in-flight nurses. More and more, the airlines' elite clientele *expected* to see glamorous single ladies on board. Thus began the era of "Coffee, tea or me? or Fly the friendly skies! or Fly the Top Banana in the sky!" These promotions lasted until the late 70s.

All the airlines competed fiercely and produced some very creative ads to entice 'the cream of the crop' into becoming 'stews'. For example, here's part of one that was used by United Airlines:

'There is no job more challenging and rewarding for a young woman than that of a stewardess because it's caring for others. Passengers from all walks of life depend on you. Every day you fly, your smile, your friendly word will bring enjoyment and relaxation to their trips. Frequently, airline hostesses are 'stolen' by unmarried passengers. To qualify, you must be responsible, attractive and personable, single, age 20 through 26, between 5'2" and 5'9", weight be in proportion to height, not to exceed 140 lbs., vision correctable to 20/30 in each eye. You can earn up to $410/per mo. and fly anywhere in the USA without cost.'

My airline was like most of the others in that it required stewardesses to have at least two years of college or two years of public contact work to get the job. Once hired, we were also required to sign an agreement to leave in the event we got married or turned thirty-two. I didn't think twice about signing it — I just wanted to get in.

Again looking back, I believe God took good care of me through the brave people who fought for resisted equality in the workplace. Within a few years, it resulted in the removal of both the 'single' and the 'age limit' rules.

In the summer of 1965, I passed ground training and completed my 'group-hands-on flight.' Now, it was time to work my first 'solo-hands-on flight,' during which I was to perform all duties of the regular stewardess while she observed me and gave me a critique if necessary.

I have vivid memories of that day. Las Vegas McCarren International Airport was baking in the summer sun.

As I entered the terminal, my nervousness was blistering too, and despite my crisp appearance, my hands were wringing wet! Although I had not officially graduated, Bonanza had given me a uniform consisting of a pale blue suit, white blouse, white hat, white gloves, black leather purse and black patent shoes. Pretty sharp!

Passing by the coffee shop, I spotted a Bonanza pilot and a fellow stewardess. Since I had time to spare, I didn't hesitate to stop to talk to them. After all, I was one of *them* now!

I walked over to their booth and asked, "Do you mind if I join you?"

"Of course not," the captain stood up and smiled, "Have a seat. You must be one of the new hires."

"Yes, I'm Bettina." Grateful for the welcome, I sighed, "I'm *so* nervous!"

As I sat there shaking, the pilot reassured me, "Just relax. The airline needs you just as much as you need them!"

I will never forget his comforting words nor the ones of the 'real' stew. Brimming with confidence, she said, "I've been flying for two years, and I really enjoy it. You get tired at times, but it's a lot of fun!"

Before long, I had to report for my flight. I thanked the helpful soon-to-be fellow crew members, and feeling less nervous, I headed towards the departure gate.

A cooperative agent opened the door leading to the sizzling tarmac. Since there were no 'jet-ways' or 'jet-bridges' connecting directly to the planes yet, I rushed across the hot pavement toward the Fairchild F-27.

The F-27, perched high on its long landing gear, was known as "Chicken Hawk" among the mechanics. They also lovingly referred to it as an "eggbeater," because it had propellers. Yet, the two propellers were attached to its two jet engines, one on each wing, making Bonanza the first all jet powered airline in the United States. It had 44 passenger seats with two doors on the left side of the plane; "forward" was the cargo door and "aft" was the entrance.

I climbed up the shaky metal stairs to enter the plane, immediately finding myself facing the tiny door concealing the lavatory, which consisted of something called a "honeybucket" — a toilet with no plumbing. To its right was an open galley area which housed a coffeemaker, cartons of beverage cans and other hospitality items such as napkins, creams and sugars, all secured by webbing. Next to the supplies were the jumpseat, phone and microphone panel and a small, open coat closet.

My observations were interrupted by a cheerful voice from the left, "Come on in and make yourself at home!" In the last row of seats sat a uniformed lady, her head buried in a newspaper, her feet propped up on a seatback. Somehow, she was also managing to hold a cup of coffee and a lit cigarette in her hands. As I approached, this pretty blonde looked up at me smiling, "Hi! I'm Kay. My supervisor told me that you'd be working your 'solo' for the Los Angeles turn. I have already been to Reno and back today, so having you is a treat. We'll be pretty full, but I'll be glad to help you out if you find you need me. Look around if you like." Then, she went back to her reading. Her relaxed mode was definitely soothing to my jangled nerves.

The first thing I did was take my jacket off because the plane's interior was as hot as an oven. Back then, cool air was not piped in or generated by a built-in ground power unit like it is now. Only after the engines were started could the cabin temperature begin to cool down. It took nearly fifteen minutes for both passengers and crew to get comfortable.

I walked up the aisle towards the front of the empty aircraft. Since Kay had taken care of tidying up, the cabin looked ready with pillows and blankets all neatly arranged in the overhead compartments. A large NO SMOKING sign was placed just above the forward door leading to the cargo area and cockpit. Smoking regulations had already changed from formerly allowing pipes, cigars and cigarettes to cigarettes only. Yes, I remember well that when I began flying in '65, passengers could smoke throughout the entire cabin. About five years later, it was restricted to the back section of the airplane and only recently have all domestic flights and some international flights become entirely smoke free.

Because I was concerned about what I would sound like over the PA system, I sat down for a minute. I wanted to review what I was about to announce and the delivery. At last it was time to board the LA bound passengers! I put on my white hat and gloves, but not the jacket since the plane's interior temperature was still steaming. I positioned myself at the door and began to greet my people cautioning the taller ones to watch their heads as I directed them into the cabin. And because seats were not yet assigned and were on a first come, first serve basis, I further offered, "Feel free to take any open seat." As soon as everyone had stowed his luggage and fastened his seat belt, the gate agent and I signaled each other that it was okay to close the stair door. Inside, near that door, was a button for me to press and hold down until the door whooshed shut. As it fell against the fuselage, I grabbed the door's huge lever and pushed downward to lock and seal it.

During the boarding process, the plane's right engine had been fired up so that the cabin's air could begin to cool. Now that the door was closed, the left engine began to roar, and we started to taxi away from the gate. It was time for my first welcome announcement and thank goodness it went off without a hitch. Then, after a last walk through to check that all was well in the cabin, I sank down onto the jumpseat to prepare for takeoff. I took that opportunity to do a silent review of emergency procedures just as I had been taught to do in ground school.

In just a few moments we were bouncing up through the summer clouds, and Las Vegas became a diminishing city below us. All too soon it was time for me to turn my attention to the preparation of my very first beverage service since training. When the NO SMOKING sign was turned off, I made the "cigarette smoking only" announcement, told the passengers that I would be by shortly with refreshments and concluded with 'Please keep your seat belts fastened since we cannot always predict air turbulence.'

I quickly switched from heels into flats for my first in-flight service. Even though we were required to change into more comfortable shoes, the pointy-toed, restrictive high heels that stewardesses were compelled to wear for years have caused many senior flight attendants, including me, to undergo corrective foot surgery.

I arranged clear plastic glasses on a serving tray, filled each one with ice and soft drinks and began my bumpy trip down the aisle. As soon as I got the hang of it and could steady myself as I offered the drinks. As I gave refills and picked up empty cups, I noticed that the cabin temperature had *finally* become much more comfortable.

After flying over the Mojave Desert and the Big Bear Mountains, we reached the seemingly endless Los Angeles suburbs. The NO SMOKING sign came back on to signal that the pilots were beginning to make their airport approach. I was astonished that it was already time for me to make the landing announcement and safety check. Forty-five minutes had literally 'flown' by with busyness!

As we taxied in, I announced our arrival and once again put on my high heels. When we finally stopped at the gate, I released the door which fell out and down, exposing the steps. I followed procedure by peeking out to make sure the rotary blades had stopped. As the passengers deplaned, I smiled and repeated the "Thank You. Bye now. I'll see you again soon. Watch your head and watch your step" speech to each and every one.

They were gone! I had done it! I was bushed. I kicked off my heels. We had just thirty short minutes before turning back to Las Vegas. There was no time to enjoy the glorious California sunshine because the cabin needed to be straightened.

The senior stewardess suggested, "Let's do this quickly, and then we can take a break." So we gathered all the pillows, put clean covers on them and returned them to the overhead racks. I collected newspapers, napkins and other trash that had been left behind. Though we both worked quickly, I barely had time to have a drink of water before we started boarding again. Once again we 'filled up' with new faces, headed for Las Vegas and arrived there in no time at all. By now, my body, and feet were looking forward to soaking in a hot tub, and so was I! Thank God my first flight's senior stewardess

142

was such a help to me that day. I'll never forget Kay's assistance on board the plane and her kindness for giving me such a good report. A few days later, my hard earned wings were pinned on my uniform jacket's lapel by one of Bonanza's officers. I was absolutely beaming, so proud that I had survived the rigors of training to be one of only nine in our original class of fifteen candidates to graduate. After the pinning, we all felt like celebrities as we posed for the local newspaper photographers' flashing cameras, recording this special moment in time for us all.

Now I was a qualified reserve stewardess and could be assigned to take a flight anytime I was on call. Airlines used the same reserve system then as they do now to satisfy the FAA regulation that a stewardess (then) or a flight attendant (now) cannot be airborne on domestic flights for more than eight hours in a 24-hour period without sufficient rest.

Right from the start I was kept quite busy filling in for stewardesses who were grounded because of 'legalities' or for illness or other unavoidable situations. Since new hires could be on reserve anywhere from one month to six years, I gladly considered myself one of the lucky ones because my reserve time turned out to be only six months.

The day after my graduation, I was already on call, wondering when the phone would ring. I didn't have to wait very long though, because two days later, it rang off the hook in the middle of the night and woke me from a very sound sleep. "Guess what? We have a flight for you." I was told to report in two hours for a 'red-eye' flight scheduled to depart for Los Angeles at 2:30 am.

"This is it!" I thought to myself, oblivious to the early morning hour because I was so excited. It took me no time at all to get ready and, before I knew it, I was rushing to the Vegas airport in the coolness of the summer night. I arrived

143

with time to spare.

Most of the passengers I greeted on my first "red-eye special" looked tired and smelled of smoke and alcohol. They went to sleep right away. I served a little coffee and some bloodymarys to the few people who stayed awake. Since it was a night flight, there was no turbulence. It was a breeze to work, and I loved it!

In LA, I had a three hour layover before returning to Las Vegas, so I headed immediately for the 'Sleep Room' that Bonanza provided for its flight crews. Even though I was only a rookie, I quickly learned to take advantage of rest periods any time and anywhere in between flights.

Besides being a reserve, I was also a probationary stewardess for the first six months subject to random performance evaluations. Supervisors could and did show up without notice on my flights to give me a "check ride", flying along to observe and report on my appearance and competency. These managers didn't miss a trick, and every time they made sure that I was wearing that all important girdle! I was checked at least once a month, sometimes twice, and I passed each time with flying colors.

My non-routine schedule and ongoing enthusiasm for my new career made the six months of probation and reserve time pass very quickly. When it ended, I was relieved and thrilled to become a permanent Bonanza employee and was permitted to join ALPA, the union that represented both pilots and stewardesses.

Even though I was no longer a probationary employee, I found that I actually liked my irregular working schedule. I loved that the streets were often ghostlike and that I was able to avoid rush hour traffic. I found it easier to shop on weekdays when the stores were almost empty. And I didn't mind working on weekends. I even loved flying major holidays because our planes weren't too crowded and the people that did fly were in a very festive mood.

Once I went off reserve, I was able to bid, according to my seniority, for a regular flight schedule. Oh how my seniority has changed over the past thirty-five years! In 1965, I was #44 out of 50 stewardesses. By the year 2002, after five mergers, I find myself at #193 out of my airline's 10,000+ flight attendants!

People often ask, "Is this your regular run?" I try to explain to them that we may end up flying the same particular trip at times but, generally, we change schedules on a monthly basis and work quite a variety of flights.

This is how it works: All bids are awarded according to seniority. In the middle of the month, attendants select their flights for the next month. There are choices to be made as to type of aircraft, where to fly and on what days. We must decide on one day trips, two day trips or trips lasting up to seven days. One day trips, or "turns," bring us back to our home base the same day. On longer trips, wherever we may be, the airline (in agreement with our union) selects, contracts with, and pays for our layover hotels.

When I first started flying, I had far less choices than today, and the bidding procedure remains essentially the same. But that's the only thing that's remained the same. Back then, we did it all by hand. Now, computers are used for everything from bidding to keeping track of flight hours and management information. In fact, most airlines now employ a centralized system, involving only computers and telephones. Gone are the days of working closely, face-to-face, with the schedulers at each base.

As nostalgic as I may be about the good ol' days, I consider my entire career a true lifeline. If it hadn't been for the protection of strong labor laws, my wings could have been clipped many times as I managed to survive five mergers. For me, each expansion was more stressful than the one before. Yet, each corporate change also gave me the opportunity to continue to grow as a person, all the while loving life in the sky — just as I had envisioned when Bonanza hired me so many years ago!

Two Las Vegas residents have started regular service as hostesses aboard Bonanza Air Lines F-27's, following three weeks of specialized training.

Bettina Elizabeth Brencher and Carolyn Joan Myers of Las Vegas were among the n i n e new stewardesses to graduate.

Chosen on the basis of poise, personality and appearance, airline hostesses are frequently "stolen" by unmarried passengers.

Classes are conducted periodically by Bonanza for new hostesses, who must be high school graduates, single, and between the ages of 21 and 27.

BETTINA BRENCHER

1965 Graduation Newspaper Article

First Summer Uniform

148

**Bonanza's Beloved Fairchild,
also known as Eggbeaters**

Ready to Welcome Flying Guests

Chapter 9

The Early Years

Early on, I tackled my new duties blissfully, still unaware of God's invisible protective wings enveloping me. I had finally found an identity and a sense of belonging at Bonanza. Rather than just being a number at a big company, I felt I was playing an important role in a growing operation that seemed like family. Pilots, hostesses, mechanics, agents, cleaners and office workers all knew each other by name, and we all worked together with enthusiasm to provide VIP service.

From 1965-67, our fleet was comprised of only fifteen F-27s, each staffed with two pilots and one stewardess. As a result, many times I found myself flying with the same pilots month after month. They became my heroes, literally taking me under their wings, carrying my suitcase and assisting me in any way they could. I knew I could count on them to keep me up-to-date about bad weather or any mechanical problems so I could, in turn, keep my passengers well informed. Our pilots' fun loving attitude helped make the long, stress filled working hours more bearable, even fun.

It turned out that many of Bonanza's pilots had flown bombing missions over Germany during WWII. Once in a while, we'd talk about that subject, and I'd kid them, "Ha, ha you missed me!" They'd grin but would never let on how their war experiences affected their lives. These former military men who became the pioneers of commercial aviation loved to fly and it showed. They seemed completely at ease at the helm of their planes, taking particular relish in customizing their PA announcements. As well as offering their own perky, welcome messages and flight information, they loved to inform our passengers about various points of interest as we flew over them.

In those early days, Bonanza, like most regional carriers, was government subsidized. We were expected to drop off and pick up the U.S. Mail in such places as Flagstaff, Prescott and the Grand Canyon, even if no passengers were boarding or deplaning. Our stops were never longer than thirty minutes. The frequent hop scotching and the light passenger loads provided both the space and the time for me to enjoy the breathtaking Southwest as it slipped by below.

Our early morning flights from Las Vegas' vast desert scape to the Grand Canyon were particularly thrilling because the Hoover Dam was in our flight path.

Each time we began to fly over it, I announced, "Hoover Dam is one of the Seven Wonders of the World. It is 726' high, and with seventeen generators, it provides hydro electric power for the states of California, Arizona and Nevada."

On one of these sunrise flights was a group of thirty-five German tourists who were abuzz with excitement about their day. They couldn't keep their eyes away from the windows for, below us, snaking between the sandy hills and rocky canyons, shimmered the deep blues and greens of Lake Mead and the Colorado River. Never one to pass up the opportunity to use my native tongue, I quickly improvised and made my sightseeing announcement in German.

The surprised and curious group of 'foreigners' asked, "Where did you learn to speak German so fluently?"

I explained that even though I had come to reside in America at the age of ten, I'd kept up with my first language by speaking it at home and studying German Lit in college. As I again used German to announce our approach to Grand

155

Canyon Airport, they all spontaneously cheered and applauded, and my heart warmed. *Das Leben ist doch wunderschoen!* Life *really* is great, I thought to myself!

My bird's-eye viewing opportunities never seemed to cease. One spring day, on a flight from the South Rim of the Grand Canyon to Cedar City, Utah, we had no passengers at all, an occurrence that didn't happen often. Just before takeoff, the captain called to suggest that I come up front where he guaranteed me a once-in-a-lifetime experience. Without hesitating, I entered the cockpit (nowadays called the flight deck), sat down on the extra pilot jumpseat and strapped myself in, ready for whatever awaited me.

As we soared away from the south plateau toward the North Rim, the plane dropped slightly downward. Immediately, I felt as if our little aircraft was being swallowed up by the immense and timeless wonder of the Canyon, aglow in the morning sun.

The captain hadn't exaggerated — I was in awe and remained that way for the duration of the flight. When we flew low over Zion National Park and Bryce Canyon, it seemed to me as if the spectacular sandstone cathedral spirals almost touched us. What a breathtaking vista it was!

Even though I preferred the smoother night and early morning flights, I often found myself on mid-day runs which, because of air currents and rising heat, were usually much more turbulent. One such trip from Las Vegas to Reno will illustrate my point. From the very start, it was a bumpy ride, and by the time we entered the space over Red Rock Canyon area, our little F-27 was really a-rocking and a-rolling. The turbulence, along with the stifling heat in the cabin, made for a lethal combination, and it didn't take long for a woman sitting in the front row to get airsick. She was the first in a domino effect of sick passengers. What a mess!

156

I knew the only thing that would keep me from joining the sickfest was to plunge head on into my duties. So I held my breath and began to provide some temporary relief to my passengers: I handed out wet towels so they could clean up; I handed out ice-cube filled paper towels so they could cool their necks and foreheads; I passed out lots of 7-Up to help soothe their nausea; and I supplied blankets to cover up the odors emanating from the floor. That day our small prop plane earned its nickname — "The Vomit Comet!" Thank goodness my pilots radioed ahead to Reno, and a cleanup crew was ready for us as soon as we landed.

Back in the mid-60s, stewardesses were subjected to a constant barrage of sexist remarks from both male passengers and airline employees. Most of us managed to paste on a smile and tried our best to ignore all the insults and bury any resentment we had.

Only once did a captain overstep his boundaries with me, and to this day, I have no idea what possessed him to do what he did. There I was in my efficient looking summer uniform — a pretty pale green skirt and a crisply starched white, short-sleeved blouse. My uniform's eye-catching feature was a Jackie-style pillbox cap which, once on my head, stayed there all day. I just kept it on because it took time to pin on the rollers hidden underneath to keep it from sliding, and it took me forever to pin that darned hat into my hair or wig.

As I was going about the business of straightening up the cabin in between flights, the captain swung open the cabin door and charged towards me. As he approached me, he reached out and put both his hands on both of my breasts. I was utterly stunned but that quickly turned to shock and anger.

I knew we were alone on the plane, and I had to do something to get him to let go. With all the strength I could muster, I pushed him away from me and gasped, "Don't do that!" The man just chuckled to himself and nonchalantly walked away. I worked the rest of the day feeling utterly embarrassed.

Later that day, I was still shaken and told two mechanics about the incident and asked if they thought I should file a complaint against the pilot. They said they knew how upset I was, and very disappointedly I heard them say, "Who would you report it to? It won't do any good to tell the chief pilot. He'll just take the pilot's side."

When I got back home, I telephoned Donna, my dear stewardess friend, and shared what had happened to me. She too was concerned about me and also advised, "Just forget about it. It doesn't make sense to stir anything up." Even though I didn't follow through with my complaint, sharing my outrage with my co-workers and friend helped dissipate some of my anger.

After the infamous incident, I tried to stay away from the offending captain, but my schedule forced me to work with him every so often. I was still very, very uncomfortable whenever he was around, but I did my best under the circumstances. Then, after a few years, I was able to avoid him completely by bidding for a different schedule. Several years later I heard that he had to retire early due to illness.

All I can say is thank goodness the majority of pilots were friendly yet professional with me. Fortunately, that day turned out to be the only negative incident with pilots.

Oh, how the pendulum has swung for female workers' rights since that time! Gradually, the image of stewardesses changed, especially after the carriers hired men as stewards.

Over time, more people with degrees and credentials

were added to our workforce and the more gender neutral professional title of "flight attendant" evolved.

Back then, rumors were rampant that flight crews were having extramarital affairs. I can only assume that some did because right after the "single" rule was dropped in 1966, a few pilots divorced and then tied the knot with their hidden stewardess girlfriends. I had secret crushes on a couple of pilots, but I never really got involved with them because either they or I had partners at the time.

Changes in the Air

I was fascinated by all the changes in the air. Late in 1965, Bonanza added two McDonnell Douglas DC-9 aircraft to its existing fleet of F-27s. DC-9s were twinjets, with one engine on each side just in front of the tail. Because they were quieter and had a bigger passenger capacity, these planes were ideal for domestic flying.

The employees couldn't wait to get acquainted with this new kid in the sky. Stewardesses were immediately trained to operate its emergency features, including the oxygen supply systems. And, as always, knowing how all the window and door exits worked under both normal and emergency conditions was a must.

Since the FAA required two stewardesses to work the new jet plane, my lone ranger flying days were over. One of us delivered the welcome announcement while the other one demonstrated the plane's safety features, showed passengers where their safety cards were located and pointed to the exits. Our demos also required that we mime how to properly use the seat belts and oxygen masks.

All eyes were on us for our new "performance", and it made me feel like I was role playing on a stage. Even though I was a little self-conscious about both my appearance and my acting at first, I learned my routine quickly, because I knew I was passing on vital safety information to my captive audience. To this day, the flight attendants are onboard for everybody's safety — frequent flyers, not-so-frequent flyers and new flyers. Personally, I use these announcements as a second "hello," because it's another opportunity to connect us, the server and the servees.

Over the years, flyers have gotten bored with our spiel. So to get their attention, I eventually got creative by using several different techniques. First, there's that all important eye contact. Sometimes, I single someone out and say directly to him or her, "I know I'm a classic! So, which do you prefer, a video or me?"

"You, of course," I usually hear.

Other times, I might tease a person whose nose is buried in a book or newspaper, "If you don't watch me, you're not getting anything to drink." The person will usually look up at me, smile and give me his full attention.

Often people mimic my movements; instead of being offended or getting upset, I think to myself, "At least they're paying attention." (Of course, after 9/11, most passengers began to pay more attention to all air travel procedures again.)

Our service procedure changed drastically on the DC-9s. At first, we continued the old way of racing down the aisle with individual trays. But this method soon proved too hectic on short flights, so collapsible carts were introduced.

Shortly after take-off, we would rush to set them up and stock their three tiers with all the supplies we would need for the beverage service. Then, with one of us at each end of the cart, we'd begin to serve in synchronicity.

Some years later, partially stocked trolleys replaced these folding carts, but we still had to add items such as ice, coffee and cups before we could begin to serve. Eventually, to save even more time, carts requiring only one attendant replaced the two person trolleys.

We were always in rush-mode on those short flights, but, somehow, we managed to get the job done! One of us discovered that starting the beverage service from the back of the airplane was much more practical because it had us going downhill, so to speak. Even though we'd usually still be serving as we began our descent, at least we'd be rolling *towards* the galley where, hopefully, we would end up just as the final approach began. Then, just before landing, one of us could secure items in the galley while the other one picked up the empty cups.

These were frantic flying times for me. For months, I flew three Las Vegas-to-Los Angeles round trips a day at least four times a week. We were at cruising altitude for only thirty-five minutes — barely enough time to serve a hundred passengers. We were so rushed that, one day, after the second round trip, my partner gave me a puzzled look as she lifted up the microphone to make the landing announcement

In all sincerity she asked me, "Is this LA or Vegas?" Thank goodness I had been keeping track! Those were certainly the good old days!

Over the years, I've been assigned to fly on increasingly bigger airplanes with their improved bells and whistles, and I've worked cross-country flights and overseas of much longer duration. Nowadays, even though there's much more to do, it seems we're not quite as rushed as we were in the early days. But one thing hasn't changed a bit: the entire cabin crew's good attitude and teamwork is still the

161

key to smooth service.

Our DC-9 fan-jets were called "fun jets" because they flew to delightful destinations like Las Vegas, Palm Springs and the beach resorts of Mexico. To enhance this image of the fast paced, fun filled jet-setter life, airlines painted their planes' exteriors with bright colors and bold patterns and provided us stews with snazzy, brightly-colored uniforms to match. In 1967, we found ourselves in orange mini dresses. By 1968, Air West let us choose which mini suited us — blue, gold or red. No matter how loud the uniforms got, at least those unmanageable hats were a thing of the past!

The outward appearance of the planes and cabin crews weren't the only changes taking place. The industry itself was expanding so quickly that sometimes it was tough to keep track. In 1968, Bonanza became Air West. Just two years later, when Howard Hughes bought us out, we turned into Hughes Air West. As more and more cities were added to our route structure and more and more people began flying, more cabin crews were needed. So, male stewards were hired to work alongside the girls.

It was also a time when the airlines began to relax some of their employee rules, allowing all stewardesses to be married, have children and wear glasses. Even the girdle and weight checks were dropped! Still unaware of my Invisible Guardian, I kept cruising along with all these changes happening in my industry - and the times.

Bonanza's New Bird

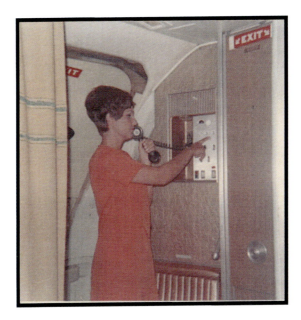

Checking PA System on DC-9

Good Times on the "Fun Jet"

Testing Megaphone on DC-9
Note the Open Overhead Bins

Chapter 10

My Airline Family

In 1968, Phoenix-based Bonanza merged with two other regional carriers, San Francisco-based Pacific and Seattle-based West Coast, to become Air West. Instantly our route structure tripled because we were now flying to over 100 cities throughout the western United States, Canada and Mexico. Even though we now had to cope with many corporate changes and the intermingling of the other two airlines' employees, everyone was excited to be aboard such a fast growing airline.

Most of Bonanza's flight crews continued to fly together after the merger. Helen, who had been one of my Bonanza friends before, now became my frequent Air West flying partner. At one point, it occurred to us to photo-document a typical two day DC-9 trip just to show what a hectic pace we were keeping. Our first day took us from Phoenix to Tucson within Arizona, then to San Diego, Los Angeles, Monterey and San Francisco in California. From there, it was on to Eugene, Oregon, then to Pasco, Washington — seven stops in all. We called these our "killer trips" because we had to rush through our duties from start to finish — greeting, serving, thanking, prepping for the next leg, greeting, serving — well, you get the picture. This hurry-up-and-wait routine amounted to over seven hours of hard flying time in a thirteen hour duty day. It was mind numbing work!

Even though these were short-hop domestic flights, I'm convinced they caused as much jet lag and fatigue as did international flights. When we finally stepped into the hotel elevator on that particular marathon trip, we all just stood there. Nothing moved. The reason: no one had remembered to push the button that would take us to our floor. When Helen realized what was going on, she just sighed and said, "I think I left my brain on the plane." As tired as we all were, the entire crew still agreed to meet for an early dinner so that we could unwind, if only for a little while.

The next day, we were up and at 'em before sunrise because we had to work that same schedule in reverse. Thanks to our great attitudes, we knew it was a do-able day, and it literally flew by. This fast pace still exists today on every airline, and it continues to cause everybody's body clock to get messed up, to say nothing of the mental and emotional toll it takes.

I can't count the times passengers have said, "How do you keep smiling all the time?" These comments of recognition for the work they observed me doing helped to soothe the aches of my body, nourish my soul and made me feel that all my rushing around was definitely worthwhile.

Many of my Air West buddies and I maintained our friendships outside the workplace, and we used any occasion as an excuse to throw a party. We celebrated our birthdays, engagements, marriages and almost every holiday together. Our social secretary was the former Chris Von Ostau, later married to a pilot as Mrs. Muryl Cole. We still exchange greetings and visits to this day.

When Helen was about to have her second daughter, she asked me, "Would you object if I name her Bettina?" Without hesitation I said, "Please, please do! Since I don't have any children, it would be such an honor for me."

Well, in June of 2002, my sweet namesake sent me a card announcing her graduation from Arizona State University, an event that filled me with almost parental pride.

Even though her mother and I now have different home bases, we stay in close touch, getting together whenever we can manage with our schedules. It turns out that children continue to be an important link among the senior stews; they have been the incentive for and have been included in many of our "family" gatherings.

In 1968, when our airline announced that stewardesses were allowed to be mothers and still fly, another flying friend, Judy, became an instant mother. We were all surprised and delighted when she proclaimed, "Guess what? I have a ten-year-old daughter!" None of us was even the slightest bit upset that she hadn't shared her secret with us before then. If she had disclosed the existence of her daughter, she would have risked losing her job. Judy and I continued to be buddies on and off the airplane for years. But one day in 1979, a mutual friend phoned to tell me that Judy had been found dead in her garage, slumped over the steering wheel of her still running car. Whether her death was accidental or not, I was shocked to lose her, and I still miss her so.

With the advent of the new policy, I found myself really admiring mothers who worked our very hectic schedules and still managed to raise their children. One of these modern day mothers was my dear friend, Ida, with whom I also flew a lot. When her son was born in 1970, she asked me to be his godmother, an offer I couldn't refuse. I was at the hospital the day Chris was born and have continued to be a part of his life all these years. My godson managed to overcome many adolescent and teenage problems and is now a proud flight attendant himself.

One way for us to solidify our family bond was to share an apartment with a fellow flight attendant. I was lucky to have a great roommate named Lucretia from Lubbock, Texas, who was more easygoing than anyone I had ever met and who had a fabulous sense of humor. Unfortunately for her, she also had a problem maintaining her weight below the company's then existing guidelines. At one point, she was given three months to pass one of our monthly weigh-ins. But, try though she might, when her deadline day arrived, she was still one pound over the restrictive limit and she was fired on the spot. She had no choice but to leave. Not only did many of us feel that we'd lost a member of our family, *I* was forced to find a new roommate!

I must include one other woman who is, to this day, still like a sister to me. Donna and I met one day in 1968 when she was pass-riding on the flight I was working from Las Vegas to Phoenix. When she introduced herself, I immediately admired her beauty and graceful manner and thought to myself, "Now, this is a stewardess with a lot of class and style!" Our lifelong friendship really began a month later when I was pleasantly surprised to run into her again at a party hosted by mutual airline friends. Though, at times, we did fly together, mostly we just exchanged dinner parties.

Then, quite coincidentally in 1972, we each bought a townhouse in the same Scottsdale subdivision. There, we had our own space and yet we were close enough neighbors to nurture our friendship. Our main bond and focus was for each of us to find 'Mr. Right' because, back then, we both thought that romance was the only way to happiness. We went about our many relationships separately, happy when they were blossoming and unhappy if they dropped their petals. Throughout all these dramas, we were there for each other. One day, Donna proclaimed, "Men may come and men may go, but our friendship will last forever!" And so it has been to this day!

As in all families, airline life was not always "up, up and away." Often, we were forced to mourn together. In 1969

175

after our airline was purchased by Howard Hughes and it became Hughes Air West, we attended many funerals. One of the saddest was for our beloved friend, Captain Walt Tubb, a man who lived for flying. He hated the FAA's policy that forced him to retire at 60. While still flying commercially, Walt had pursued his fun hobby of aerobatics and had even become Arizona's state champion. So, after his mandatory retirement, he continued living his passion for three more years. Then, while performing at an air show in Arizona, he made a low loop from which he couldn't pull up. His little plane dove into the ground, killing him instantly. Both his family of origin and his extended airline family were in total shock because everyone had loved this dear man. It was a sad day indeed when we all gathered around his Scottsdale gravesite to send him off to pilot heaven.

1971 was a very sad time for me because one of our DC-9s collided in mid-air with a Phantom fighter jet. While doing its loops, the military aircraft pierced our plane at the forward passenger entrance and galley area. Somehow, the DC-9 didn't catch fire. It just dropped from the air and landed like a flattened pancake in the unpopulated rolling hills just outside Los Angeles. Everyone on board perished. All Air West employees shared in this loss.

That wasn't the end of the funerals. There was one for Susie, a stewardess in her late 30s who died of liver cancer. Another stewardess, Markie, was killed along with her husband in a horrific head-on car crash on a central Arizona highway. They were both riding in the back seat of another couple's car, and they died hugging each other. Mr. and Mrs. Lynch were buried in one casket — still hugging each other.

Alongside my airline family, I learned life lessons that would serve me well as I began my spiritual quest.

From left: friend Ida, Air West Agent, friend Donna, and Bettina

Bettina (left) fellow Airline Stewardesses

Bettina (sitting) with friend, Helen

Mid 80's - Bettina (right) with friend, Marsha

Chapter 11

Fear of Flying

Ever since I started flying, I've loved it so much that, at least most of the time, I haven't had any room in my heart or mind for fearing it. Since I've always felt so at home both with people and with soaring in the air, I couldn't quite understand why not every air traveler felt the same. But in the middle 80s, my eyes were opened to just how really scared some people are of riding in the skies even under normal conditions. After I had moved to Scottsdale, every week I went to see a woman named Linda for a manicure. It didn't take us long to become friends. One day she confided to me, "I could *never* do the work you're doing because I'm too scared to fly. Every time I've had to do it, it's been unavoidable. I've had to force myself to get on that plane because I didn't want to mess up our family's vacation. I really don't know why I freeze up, but *I just don't feel comfortable in an airplane.* Even when we're cruising along smoothly, I get anxious, I have trouble breathing and my whole body tightens up."

At the time, I just couldn't fathom what she meant. "It's hard to understand, Linda, and it's a shame because you're missing out on a lot of fun, like enjoying all the amazing scenery below." Linda agreed, "Yeah, but I can't help the way I feel. I hope that, when I do have to fly again, I'll get a friendly stewardess like you because I sense you really try to make everyone feel comfortable." I thanked her, but I couldn't help that I was puzzled about her problem.

Six months later, I was at her salon again when something came up that gave me a clearer understanding about the fear she experienced when she flew. As she was polishing my nails, I happened to glance down under her table where I spotted a big bug crawling close to my left foot. I just about hit the ceiling, screaming, "Get that bug away from me!" Calmly, Linda looked for a jar, captured the bug and carried it outside to freedom. Soon she was back in her chair with her head down, working on my nails, seemingly deep in thought. Even so, she could see that it was taking me quite a while to recover from my panic.

"*Now*, maybe you can understand how *I* feel about flying," she told me. "I react to it like you just reacted to that poor cricket. You have a hard time understanding that it's harmless." That episode at the salon helped me to be more compassionate with all the phobic folks I met, especially my fearful flyers. From then on, I have spent even more time with the nervous ones. I worked hard to assure them, "This airplane is really quite safe. All the noises you're hearing are normal. I've done this for a long time and *I'm* still here! Maybe it'll help you be less edgy if you compare this plane to a boat in the water. When the water's smooth the boat just glides along; when the water's rough the boat rocks a little, but there's really nothing to worry about. Air currents affect an airplane in the same way — when you feel a few bumps, there's really no danger."

Chatting with them is the basic tool I employ to help my panicky guests switch their fearful thoughts to more pleasant ones. "So, where are you heading today? Are you on vacation or off to visit relatives?" I ask. Sometimes I gently touch their arm and suggest that they take a few deep breaths to try to relax a bit. Then, when they look up at me and manage a smile, I know I've accomplished my mission.

But, still, I usually keep my eye on them until we've landed. Knowing I have made *them* feel a little better makes *me* feel so much better.

Sometimes, though, the tables are turned when my passengers ask me if *I'm* afraid of flying. To this specific question I always answer honestly with an emphatic *no.* I explain that I'm either enjoying myself too much or I'm too busy with my duties to think about anything else. In hindsight, I'm glad I haven't been consumed with "angst" as I've worked all these years, because I would have missed the joy of the present moment.

Fearful Experience

I always give a different answer if the question is rephrased to, "Are you ever scared?" That's when I answer, "You bet I am, sometimes." Because the truth is that I still get frightened in really bad weather conditions. For example, I do tend to tense up whenever we must make an instrument approach in foggy weather. That situation seems to take forever and the suspense just kills me. And, at times, storms make me hold my breath. I don't like the thunder, the lightning or the severe turbulence that usually accompany them. These are the times when I myself turn into a "white knuckle flyer" — when I hold on to my jumpseat and pray to the God that I had ignored for so long to please guide the pilots a little more than usual. Thank goodness this doesn't happen too often!

Those same pilots I rely on and pray for aren't ever very open about their own fears. If an approach seems to me to have been more 'hairy' than usual, I try to pry information out of them.

"That landing was pretty busy for you, wasn't it?" I casually say.

"Yeah, we had a strong crosswind," is the typical comment I get. Most of them tend to stick to the facts, never revealing what's really going on inside them. I experienced *my* scariest turbulence ever in March of 1988! Even though thunderstorms were hovering everywhere that morning, we were cleared for takeoff from the Memphis airport, destination Jackson, MS. My pilots requested that, until they notified us further, everyone including flight attendants remain seated with belts securely fastened. After I gave a quick check to see that all my people were tucked in securely, I headed for my jumpseat at the back of the plane.

Right after takeoff, our little DC-9 began to shake violently. The second I felt it, I scrambled out of my jumpseat and headed for a seat in the last unoccupied row because, for some reason, it made me feel a little better to be able to look out a window. Outside, the sky was dark gray and green; inside that cabin, it was dark as night and rocking worse than any roller coaster I'd ever been on. We were jerking every which way at once — to the left, to the right, up and down! I found myself pulling my seatbelt tighter and clutching the armrest, just like all those panicky flyers whom I had attempted to calm over the years. I began to silently scream in terror.

Suddenly, the eerie silence that enveloped the cabin was interrupted by the driving rain pounding on the plane's exterior skin. The drumming outside reverberated inside as the plane continued bouncing around aimlessly in the angry sky. Then, after ten more agonizing minutes — an eternity — over the PA came the pilot's calm and reassuring voice, "We apologize for the bumpy ride. Due to the weather conditions, it took us a little longer than scheduled, but we'll be landing in Jackson shortly." Just as he had reassured us, we did land safely. As my passengers silently deplaned, each one grateful to be on solid ground, I thanked God for taking care of us all because, miraculously, not one person had been hurt.

After everyone had left, I rushed into the cockpit and said to the pilots, "That was the roughest ride I've ever had!" The captain, who was calmly going over his after-landing checklist, didn't say a word. But the co-pilot said, "I've got to agree with you, Bettina. That's the worse turbulence I've had to tackle in the twenty years I've been flying."

Later that evening, safe at home, I switched on the news and saw that day's weather reported as the lead story! It turns out that a tornado had been spotted at the very time we'd been bouncing around in the air on our way to Jackson. No wonder our flight crew couldn't find any smooth pockets to fly in to escape the storm!

Close Calls

Sometimes I get this question: "Have you ever had any close calls?" "I've had at least two," I reply and, if there's time, I elaborate. The first one was in 1970 on a flight from Puerto Vallarta to Phoenix. Just after takeoff, a man in the Mexican control tower started screaming over our cockpit's radio in broken English, "Something fall off from your aeroplane! A wheel comes off!" Despite that desperate warning, the captain decided to remain on course for Phoenix and have the tower there check our landing gear. At the same time he made this decision, he let the cabin crew know that we needed to prepare for an emergency landing. We then informed our passengers, who listened carefully, so that they could follow our instructions.

Once we got over Phoenix, we made a fly-by for the air traffic controllers to check us out. They confirmed that all the plane's wheels were intact and down and concluded that, instead of an entire wheel, only one tire's outer rubber had come off in Mexico. Still, as a precaution, we circled the airport to burn off fuel before we landed. With emergency vehicles and fire trucks lining both sides of the runway, we managed that landing without any problems, much to everyone's relief. The instant we touched down, the false calm that had been pervasive throughout the flight vanished. Everyone on board broke into spontaneous applause, giddy with their good fortune.

I experienced another close call one January night in 1976. Oddly enough, it too began at Phoenix Sky Harbor International Airport. Our take off for the flight to California's Orange County Airport was normal, and our initial climb went very smoothly. But, unfortunately, it didn't stay that way for long. Just as I began to walk towards the forward galley to help my partner set up the beverage cart, I heard a loud bang outside the cabin. At that exact moment, we suddenly dipped to the right and I was thrown completely off balance. As I braced myself against a seat back for support, the DC-9 slowly began to level off and all appeared to be normal once again. But all the passengers had heard that loud clank and had felt the plane's sudden shift, so everyone was quite alarmed.

As I was rushing back to pick up my interphone, the captain's voice came over the PA, saying, "Apparently, we've had a problem, but we don't yet know the exact nature of it. As a safety precaution, we are reducing our power and turning back to Phoenix."

With quick and quiet resolve, my partner and I prepared the cabin for landing, while at a very slow speed it seemed as if we were suspended motionless in midair and as if we might fall out of the sky at any moment. Once again, as we touched down safely, our passengers' sighs of relief mingled with our own.

Little did they know how close a call it had actually been! When the mechanics checked out our plane, they found that part of the right engine's cover— cowling — had been ripped off. If this loose part had hit the vertical stabilizer while we'd been aloft, the pilot would have lost control of the aircraft and a crash would have been inevitable.

I guess flying could be compared to childbirth because I soon forgot about this scary incident and returned to the routine of my flying work, confident that I was as safe there as any other work place.

Chapter 12

People Who Love People

Barbara Streisand's *People* has always been my career's theme song. Here's the reason: No matter how gloomy my private life was, my love for the flying public always inspired me to keep going. Although I'm not so gloomy anymore, the theme song holds true for me to this day. The fact that I get the chance to serve "my" passengers, even for a short time, still gives me the feeling that I *am* indeed the luckiest person in the world.

I look forward to every flight because I know it will give me the opportunity to meet people from all walks of life, every age and size, and many nationalities. Often, just before they come aboard, the plane's empty cabin reminds me of a chapel's quiet hush before its service. When it's time to welcome our passengers, I usually glance in a mirror for a last minute personal appearance check as I await the signal from the gate agent or the lead flight attendant, who inform the cabin crew with a loud and clear, "Here they come!"

But before that moment, it takes an entire team to get ready to give our visitors a good flying experience. Workers fill the aircraft with the right amount of fuel, mechanics check the log books, ground personnel load suitcases and other cargo, cleaners straighten up the cabin and caterers board service supplies. While the co-pilot goes on his visual 'walk around' outside the aircraft, flight attendants meet to bid for their cabin positions and to check the emergency equipment in their designated areas. Then all the flight attendants meet with the captain for a final briefing.

I've had the honor to meet and serve many "special needs" individuals over the years, and many have touched me in a profound way. One cold November night in 1999, on a flight from Memphis to Kansas City, our customer service agent informed us that we were pre-boarding one such physically challenged passenger. As I waited at my mid-cabin greeting spot, a gentleman came on carrying a petite woman in his arms. He walked to 5B and gently placed her in the seat. When he left to get their carry-on luggage from the jetway, I walked over to greet her.

"Hi! How are you this evening?" I asked. "It looks like you two have done this many times and have your routine down pat." She just smiled at my comment and nodded.

As soon as they were settled in, we began our general boarding. Later, when we'd finished our beverage service and I was picking up 'empties,' I took the time to stop and chat once more. For some reason, we just clicked and I felt comfortable enough to jump head-on into a discussion about overcoming my own childhood trauma. Both of them seemed to understand and accept what I was saying. After I shared my story, the woman told me that she had multiple sclerosis, and we talked about that for a little bit. But once again duty called, and I left to prepare for landing. My friendly couple was the last to deplane. I was surprised to see that the woman was waiting for me in the jetway as I walked through the plane's door. She called me over to her and pulled out a book from a basket attached to the back of her personal scooter. As she handed it to me, she said, "I wrote this and think you may find this quite interesting, Bettina."

It was only after we had said our goodbyes that I looked at the book's cover. It was entitled *You Are Not Your Illness* by Linda Noble Topf, M.A. When I finally had the chance to read her memoir, I treasured her story of how she had moved from victim to victor in her effort to deal with her MS. At that time, writing my own memoir was just a seed in my mind, but her book inspired me to keep on nurturing the idea, so I eventually began to write my own book.

One of the "passengers-coming-aboard-games" that I enjoyed playing over the years is "silent detective." To myself I would think, "Are you a new flyer or a frequent one? Are you flying for business or are you on vacation? Where are you from?" Sometimes I'd get the answers during the flight but even if I didn't, I enjoyed playing the guessing game.

First time flyers of all ages were the most fun for me. Parents always let me know that their children were firsttimers. If the little one was a baby, I'd give our honorary wings to the mother or father. If it was an older child, I'd present him or her with the wings directly, along with the First Flight Certificate. As I handed the mementos to these youngsters, I always performed a ritual that another flight attendant had started a few years back. I'd ask the young rider to raise his or her right hand and repeat after me: "I (they'd state their name) promise to have a good time, now and every time I fly on your airline." At first, they'd be somewhat surprised, but after the little ceremony, both the kids and their parents were delighted. If time permitted after we'd landed, these curious and newly awarded kids even got to visit the cockpit and meet the pilots.

Most mature first timers either announce that it's their first flight or I recognize them by their excitement and/or nervousness. But one time I didn't realize that I had a first time flyer aboard until she was about to deplane.

Throughout the entire flight, she sat quietly and serenely in her seat and had given me a little smile every time I came by. Only as I assisted my sweet elderly passenger to her wheelchair did she confess to me "I'm 93 years old and this was my first time to try flying. It sure took me long enough! But it's not bad at all. I may just do it again soon!"

Then there was the time when a family entourage announced that they were taking their 70 year old mother who had never flown before on a Caribbean cruise. Three of us flight attendants immediately began to fuss over her, "Welcome aboard. Just relax. We hope you enjoy the flight."

After the breakfast service, we presented her with her very own wings and photographed her whole gang. 'Mama' started to feel more comfortable and exclaimed with childlike enthusiasm, "I didn't know flying could be so much fun!" Her excitement rubbed off on passengers and crew alike, and her family was delighted with the attention we gave her.

I always give unaccompanied children special treatment in addition to what is required by FAA and corporate regulations. I introduce myself and explain the plane's safety features to each one. Then, I help them get settled in their seats and ask them some basic questions. "What's your name? Would you like your bag under the seat or up in the compartment? Where are you going? Who's meeting you? Do you fly a lot? Do you know what kind of plane you're on?" It's imperative for everyone to be aware of these solo youngsters, so I inform the people seated around them and the other flight attendants. At the end of each flight, I ensure that the young travelers are transferred safely to an airline representative or to the welcoming arms of whoever is supposed meet them at the airport.

I once asked an unaccompanied 6 year old boy one of my usual questions, "Have you ever flown before?"

With a very serious look on his face, he answered, "Yes, I have, a long time ago. But I don't remember anything because I was still in my mommy's tummy!"

All the unaccompanied children I've met have been

precious to me, but one really made me feel like I was touched by an angel. It happened on an afternoon flight from Anchorage to Seattle when our "lead" informed me that a little eight year old boy would be seated in my section. She also let me know that he had just been in Anchorage for his father's funeral. During that flight, I noticed that he focused on looking out the window, so I took a moment to lean over and ask him, "Aren't those pretty clouds?"

He completely ignored my question. Instead, with utter certainty, he pointed to the sky outside the window and said, "That's where heaven is, and that's where my daddy lives now."

"You're right, that's heaven," I agreed with him. I only hoped that *that* thought was comforting to him.

With tears in my heart and eyes, I related the boy's story to a pass-riding uniformed pilot who happened to be sitting in the row behind him. He insisted on moving up to sit alongside the sad child. "I have two boys myself. Maybe I'll know what to say and do." And he did! For the remainder of the flight, they played games together and once, as I walked by their seats, the boy beamed a smile my way, and I saw that he was proudly wearing the pilot's cap. That day, our plane was just a little closer to God.

Power of Compliments

Over the years, some passengers have written to my airline to thank us for the good service. I've saved some of those complimentary statements to remind me that 'up there' I've often helped my flyers to have a more memorable trip. Business travelers particularly enjoy our cheerful attitude.

One frequent flyer wrote:

May 19, 1970 . . . "I'm often able to get ahead of my competitors if I emerge from a flight in a pleasant frame of mind. This happens because gals like Helen and Bettina really put forth their greatest efforts to please the passenger so that he feels wonderful and carries that feeling with him to his contacts that day.."

Here's a note from a not-so-frequent flyer:
March 5, 1998 . . . "In coach seating we had the most pleasant and accommodating Flight Attendant [FA]. I don't fly often but I just wanted you to know how well she represented service and made the 'skies more friendly."

Passengers starting their vacations are easy to spot by their casual dress and their enthusiasm which tends to spread like wildfire:

December 1, 1981. "Our compliments to one of your cabin attendants, Bettina. There were four in our group and she took photos for each of us. She even joined us in a friendly game of cards. She certainly made the time pass enjoyably and quickly on a very long flight. Bettina is a definite asset to your airline. Her attitude and responsiveness could serve as an example for all flight attendants."

Another passenger flying to Mexico wrote:

July 7, 1973 . . . "We were traveling with four adults and six young children on the way to our vacation. The 'girls' (flight attendants) were very attentive and most wonderful with the children. They asked the captain to autograph a drawing of the plane that my son made. This was just one of the niceties accorded us. In our opinion, you can be justly proud of this crew. They provided excellent public relations."

Usually, I can easily identify returning vacationers, all suntanned and sad as they drag themselves to their seats. When I ask them, "How was your vacation? Going home now?" Their replies are always the same, "Vacation was great, but now it's back to the old routine."

Obviously, when a family or group flies together, they want to sit together. Even though seats are assigned at the time reservations are made, some of these people find themselves separated when the aircraft is filled, and they tend to get quite annoyed. On jumbo jets, re-arranging passengers is difficult to accomplish. But on the smaller, narrow body planes that I most often work on, I do my best to help out. Once, a man handed me a note when he deplaned:

June 27, 1996 . . ."I am in the U.S. Air Force and traveling with my family. I want you to know that I noticed how you took the time to co-ordinate seat assignments so we could all sit together. Solving seating duplications and making the extra effort to accommodate any

*passengers' needs are all signs of a person
who genuinely cares for others."*

At other times, my passengers have been on more serious missions. They're easy to spot because of the solemn look on their faces. Some have been on their way to funerals and some have been escorting the remains of loved ones. I've always tried to be of comfort to them in whatever small ways I could.

One such traveler remains vivid in my memory. In 1995, on a morning flight from Oklahoma City to Memphis, I noticed a middle-aged man who sat there wringing his hands and staring out the window. He looked as if he was in shock. To give him a chance to share, I asked him if everything was okay. He answered slowly and without much emotion, "They called me last night and told me my boy died yesterday in a house fire. I'm a truck driver. I'm going back to bury him."

What else could I say besides "Oh, I'm *so* sorry. What's your name?"

"Ken," he replied.

"How old is your boy, Ken?" I couldn't bring myself to say "was."

"He's 4," he said, as he pulled out a picture from his wallet and handed it to me. It was a snapshot of his little son, grinning from ear to ear. I looked at the photo for awhile and felt the tears rolling down my cheeks. The father just looked down, silently lost in his memories.

I stayed with him for a few moments more, making small talk about his transfer in Memphis and his eventual destination. When he deplaned, he thanked me. I told him I'd pray for him and his family and said goodbye to yet another passenger with whom I'd had the opportunity to connect.

Airlines are also required to take special care of animals. Small pets can be put in a carrier under the seat, but most are placed in the cargo compartment; then their owners are informed that their pets are on board. Since I'm an animal lover as well as a people lover, I've had a lot of fun with passengers who've brought their pets along for the ride.

In February, 1998, I handed a female passenger her "pets are on board" notice and relayed the message that they were safe and sound in the cargo section. "By the way, what kind of pets are they?" I asked as an afterthought.

She quickly told me that her traveling companions were two cats named Caesar and Cleopatra.

"I like those names. Where are you taking them?"

"All the way to Africa," she sighed.

"Wow, that's a long way," I commented. Because I knew that many countries require animals arriving from abroad be quarantined, I was curious about her kitties, "Do Caesar and Cleopatra have to be placed in quarantine?" I was surprised to hear that they weren't facing that ordeal.

I shared with her that I'd been a dog lady but had converted to a cat lady because of Woody and Stuffy, who'd been my kitty pets for six years. I told her how wonderful they were and that they'd taught me so much. Then I said, "Well, since you have such a long trip ahead of you, I'll let you relax now."

With both of us just smiling to ourselves, thinking about our 'little humans in fur' (as Oprah refers to them), I moved on to my other duties.

Then in January, 1999, I was flying from Seattle to Memphis when I noticed a couple who appeared quite anxious. "Are you OK?" I asked.

"Well, *we* are but our cat *isn't,*" they fretted, pointing to the pet carrier under the seat in front of them. "Our cat is diabetic, and there's something wrong with her. We need to give her some medication, but we aren't sure how to go about it here."

I gave them a little cup of water to use, and it must have worked because, when I looked in on them later, they gave me a thumbs up and told me that their cat seemed to be better and was now resting. Later, they even wrote a thank you note:

> *"Recently, we were traveling with our 19-year-old cat when she went into diabetic shock. Our flight attendant was wonderful! She helped us way beyond the call of duty. She is kind, efficient and gives a whole new meaning to 'quality customer service.' I'm glad to say Toby survived! Rest assured, we'll always fly your airline. Thank you!!!"*

Employees Appreciate Each Other

In addition to complimentary letters from my pleased passengers, I've always appreciated it when I've gotten favorable reports from my supervisors. They would often show up unannounced to ride along and check out the safety methods, appearance and service techniques of the cabin crew.

Here are a few reports from before and after my airline's mergers:

> *April 13, 1971 . . "Your interest in being an excellent hostess for our airline is evident in every phase of your job performance. You have good rapport with your passengers and seem to enjoy pleasing them . . . ."*

> *May 11, 1972 . . . "APPEARANCE: Hairstyle practical for flight duties, becoming to you! Makeup fresh. PASSENGER CONTACT: Excellent. You have a friendly cheerful manner while performing your duties. . .creating a pleasant atmosphere for all."*

> *January 13, 1993 . . . "AIRCRAFT: Boeing 757. This team appeared to work well together. They all pitched in to help where needed. Bettina handles herself with great confidence. She obviously knows her job well--and it shows."*

At times we'd also receive compliments from other airline employees. This one came from a flight attendant with the carrier that had just purchased us:

> *November 26, 1986 . . . "The three cabin crew members were extremely polite and gracious upon boarding. The service was supreme and they should be commended. They are an asset to our airline and I look forward to working with them."*

A Customer Service Manager wrote:

> *September 28, 1988 . . . "I have written letters concerning the poor service given by our flight attendants, so I feel it's only fair to write letters about FAs who do excellent service. Two such ladies worked a flight I took recently. Their service both in first class and the main cabin was excellent. Their attitudes and professionalism were 'top shelf.' They smiled, joked with the passengers and generally left a very nice impression."*

At times, even I wrote to my company to praise a fellow flight attendant:

> *March 19, 1998 . . . "Ken was so very helpful in creating a smooth flight. It didn't surprise me at all to learn that he builds model airplanes in his spare time, because I get the sense that he truly enjoys every aspect of the airline industry. His positive attitude and enthusiasm are reflected in his interactions with customers and co-workers alike. He is a definite asset for our airline."*

> *September 1, 2000 .. "I received a most warm welcome from Kristine and Bret. They worked a smooth, professional flight and extended sincere courtesy to everyone."*

Even though these letters aren't necessary, they sure boost our crew morale and make our lives (both on planes and off) more rewarding. The compliments helped me throughout my many years of flying, to deal with the one 'complainer' that seems to appear on every flight. Letters honoring people multiply in ways we may never hear of. It is good to give thanks, is it not?

Oh yes, it's been my experience that flight crews beam with pride knowing that our airline guests are pleased with our service. When our deplaning passengers seize the moment to say goodbye with kind words such as 'Thanks for a good, safe ride.' or 'Great service!' — Well, it really makes our day!

Chapter 13

Famous People

Throughout my years of flying, passengers have not only been curious about the specifics of my job, but many have also wanted me to tell them about any famous folks that were on my flights.

"Oh yes, I've hosted many celebrities, especially when I first started flying," I say. And then, if time permits, I begin my *List of Famous Folks Who've Flown With Me* with the story of my first 'superstar.'

It was 1971, and I was on a flight from Phoenix to Orange County Airport serving Santa Ana, California. When I walked up to assist Helen, I found her smiling big, even for her, barely able to contain her excitement. "Guess who just pre-boarded? John Wayne!"

"No way!" I gasped.

"Just look in the first row!" she whispered.

Sure enough, sitting by the window, decked out in cowboy attire, was the *Duke*, flashing his famous smile my way and saying a friendly "Howdy Ma'am!" He looked so like he did on the big screen — like he'd just jumped off his horse and into Seat 1A!

As I approached this familiar stranger, my heart was pounding so hard that I could barely squeeze out, "It's an honor to have you on board."

Again he grinned warmly, but this time he was looking right at me. "Thank you, Ma'am," he said, and I could feel myself melting right there on the spot.

All too soon we were interrupted when other passengers began to board. I had no choice but to leave him

208

to greet the newcomers. As you can imagine, it didn't take long before some of them asked, "Isn't that John Wayne up front?" I guess he was pretty hard to miss in all his Western splendor!

"That's right! Isn't it great?" I exclaimed.

After we were in the air and had finished serving drinks, a gentleman approached me to check if it was at all possible to get the Duke's autograph for his son. Even though we usually respected a celebrity's privacy, I told him that I would see what I could do, because I was looking for an excuse to chat with him again myself.

Mr. Wayne was talking with his neighbor when I got to his seat, so I said, "I'm really sorry to interrupt, but there's a man in the back who would just love to have your autograph for his son."

"Why sure," he said without hesitating. "What's his name?"

It was then I realized that, in my excitement, I'd forgotten to get it, so off I went to coach. When I got back, the Duke obliged me with his signature and another big smile. And when I delivered that precious slip of paper to the grateful dad, everyone around him applauded.

Six months later, I had the Duke on another flight to Orange County Airport, which turned out to be quite near where he lived. Once again he charmed me and everyone aboard by his presence. It certainly didn't surprise me that soon after John Wayne's death, they renamed his home airport in his honor.

But John Wayne hadn't been my first flying celebrity. In the late 60s, a few years before I met the Duke, I had the pleasure of hostessing a couple also known 'round the world — Roy Rogers and Dale Evans. I wasn't aware that Apple

Valley, one of our scheduled California stops, was where they lived until they boarded my plane one day and saddled down in first class. Both of them turned out to be quite friendly; and they spent much of the flight talking with passengers and crew alike.

When "The King of the Cowboys" died in 1998, one of his sons spoke during a televised tribute. He told us all how proud he was that his father tamed the Wild West and caught the bad guys in the movies. In contrast, he did a wonderful job of lovingly teaching his children (both natural and adopted) his own steadfast values.

From my brief encounter with the man and from what I learned about him that day on television, I had to agree that he had indeed been a hero in real life as well as onscreen. So I silently hummed 'Happy Trails to you until we meet again, Mr. Rogers.'

From the late 60s through the mid 70s, I often worked the Burbank-Las Vegas route, so I got to hostess many casino showroom head liners as well as other showbiz personalities.

One day, George Burns came on board. The minute he saw me, he grinned his famous squinty-eyed grin, pointed at his cigar and proudly told me, "I know, I know — cigarettes only. It's not lit, I'm just holding it."

"Thanks for telling me that, Mr. Burns," I replied, all the while thinking to myself, "What an adorable man!"

Back in those days, Don Rickles, the sarcastic comedian, traveled with us often. Though he was never all that talkative, he was always polite. Years later, I was tickled to see that familiar bald head of his featured in a very funny carpet commercial.

On another Burbank to Las Vegas flight, young Peter Billingsley, star of *The Christmas Story*, pre-boarded as an unaccompanied minor. He looked at me with those big blue "you'll shoot your eyes out" eyes the entire time I was explaining the safety features to him. For the whole flight, he had those same baby blues focused on a book he had brought along to read. From then on, whenever he appeared in TV commercials, I was happy to see him again.

Jim Nabors once took a flight I was working. At the time, I only knew him as the lovable Gomer Pyle. I didn't know what a beautiful voice he was blessed with until years later when I bought two of his gospel tapes on sale at my local car wash. Each time I play them, I'm moved by his voice and inspired by the songs he chose to include on those tapes. I wish I could have told him how talented he was.

Sometime in the early 70s, I worked a charter flight out of Burbank Airport. The plane was chock-full of celebrities on their way to Vegas for a charity benefit that night. Front row, right side was occupied by one of the most upbeat and interactive couples I've ever seen — Steve Allen and Jayne Meadows. Just opposite them sat Florence Henderson, looking just as radiant then as she still does today.

A few rows behind them sat Laugh-In's Arte Johnson looking *verrrrry interesting* indeed— as he kept rotating his head like a periscope in search for his friends.

Ed McMahon, then Johnny Carson's longtime sidekick, seemed more than content to be sitting between the two beautiful women who were accompanying him that day.

Among this lively bunch of thirty-five were several game show hosts and other major and minor celebs, some of whom I recognized and some of whom I didn't. Even so, I was delighted to 'hobnob' with them as I went about serving drinks. I'll admit it: as far as I was concerned, this particular flight went by way too fast!

As fate would have it, I once hosted and served Joan Rivers on a flight from Las Vegas to San Jose, CA. At the

211

time, she was an up and coming comedienne who was really sarcastic and loved to skewer stewardesses in her routines. So my co-worker and I were on our guard as soon as we heard that she and her husband were flying with us that day.

When I got to their row with my beverage cart, Ms. Rivers' beleaguered Edgar did all the talking while she kept her head buried in a newspaper. I had gotten off pretty easily, but she certainly lived up to her reputation by not acknowledging my co-worker's greeting when she boarded. Instead she looked away and rushed past her as quickly as she could. Yet, over the years, I continued to admire this talented lady for some reason, despite her seeming disdain for my chosen profession.

Sometime in 1998, she apparently seemed to have had a change of heart. On one of her many talk show appearances, she redeemed herself with veteran flight attendants everywhere (whom she had continued to refer to as stewardesses). In the midst of talking about her daughter Melissa's wedding, she abruptly changed the subject, saying, "I have to share an experience I had when I was flying recently. I *must* tell this story because I've made so much fun of *flight attendants* in the past and now I'd like to give them credit for the work they are doing."

"About a month ago, I got *very* frightened on a plane that was flying through lots of turbulence. The flight attendants were amazing! They were so professional as they went about helping everyone — especially me — to calm down. So, I just want them to know I'm gonna be flying with a new attitude from now on."

I hear you, Ms. Joan Rivers, and I accept your apology. Thanks for your sincerity. I felt like you were speaking to me personally.

In the early 70s, the dashing actor George Hamilton

212

boarded a full flight from L.A. to Tucson at the last minute and had to take an aisle seat. My partner Linda and I were all aflutter as we schemed to get our picture taken with him. That involved serving everyone as quickly as we could, which we did. Linda then dug out the camera that she always carried with her for just such an occasion.

Boldly, we asked if he would let us take a picture with him. Just as boldly he said he would and, indeed, he graciously did. The photo of Linda and me with that tanned and handsome man occupies a special place in one of my many scrapbooks.

Hmmm, what's the likelihood that he'll ever show up on a flight of mine again? I wouldn't mind having an updated photo with him because I think he has an even more commanding presence now with his graying mane, perpetual tan and spiritually mellow demeanor.

Another celeb who flew with us was Lynda Carter. This *Wonder Woman* accompanied by a charming man, flew first class — a fitting place for someone as sweet and beautiful as she was and still is.

Robert Vaughn was aboard one very short and very full flight of mine. I was so busy that I barely had time to say a brief hello, but it was exciting just to serve coffee to "The Man from U.N.C.L.E."

I also got to have a very brief encounter with *Maverick* himself, James Garner, on a flight from La Paz, Mexico to Phoenix. Since he looked quite exhausted, all I did was hand him a pillow and a blanket. He thanked me, positioned his lanky body as comfortably as possible and was soon fast asleep.

Carl Sagan was my passenger once on a 45 minute flight from Las Vegas to Phoenix. The plane was packed, so he was squeezed between two people in the last row of seats.

We were barely able to get to his row to serve drinks before the plane began its descent. But when I finally got there, I said, "Aren't you . . .?"

". . .Carl Sagan," he finished my question for me.

As brief as this moment was, I was a bit in awe of the man with the great mind who had introduced us all to "billions and billions of stars."

When George McGovern ran for president in 1972, I worked a charter flight filled with his staff and some journalists who were covering his campaign. The plane's atmosphere was relaxed and casual, so when I walked into the galley, I wasn't at all surprised to find a man helping himself to a soft drink. What surprised me was that my "soda pop pilferer" was none other than Bob Schieffer, who at the time was a correspondent for CBS News.

Since I recognized him, I said, "You're Bob Schieffer, aren't you?"

"Not to be confused with Bob Shaefer, the other reporter. My last name is spelled S C H I E F F E R."

"Well, you know, I was born in Germany and I tend to recognize German names. Thanks for the clarification and it's wonderful to meet you," I said as he left the galley and returned to his seat. Now, when he appears on *Face the Nation*, the CBS evening news, or any other program, I think about our brief, but friendly conversation.

One early morning, while flying over Palm Springs, I paused near a passenger who was turned sideways in his seat, looking out the window at the amazing landscape. Even though I didn't notice who he was right away, for some reason I felt compelled to comment on the beauty of the desert in the morning sun. It was not until he looked up at me with his warm smile that I realized who he was.

"Mr. Kuralt, I didn't know it was you!" I blurted out.

214

"Isn't it beautiful out there?"

What a question to ask of that gentle man who'd invited all of us to enjoy so many of nature's wonders with him during his years at CBS's *On The Road with Charles Kuralt*.

After only a moment, I said, "Well, I'll move on and let you enjoy the view. Nice having you on board." I left him and found an empty seat where I too took a moment to look out the window and behold the beautiful world below.

Do you recall the "Battle of the Sexes" tennis match between Billie Jean King and Bobby Riggs that got so much publicity in September of 1973? Well, right after the event, the cocky little man himself came aboard, still wearing his tennis garb and carrying a racket. I guess he needed even more attention because he proceeded to remain in the aisle, pirouetting and pointing his tennis racket skyward in a victorious gesture. Funny, I recall that he got soundly trounced by Billie Jean, but I guess he still felt like a winner because he'd made a lot of money even in defeat. That bantam Bobby spent the entire ride yakking to other passengers who, like myself, seemed to enjoy having a brush with someone famous.

In 2001, I happened to catch a TV movie about the events leading up to and including the match, and I was reminded of the uproar it had caused at the time. Commenting on her reasons for accepting the challenge to play Bobby Riggs, Billie Jean King said that the 70s women's movement had given her all the motivation she needed. "I realized that my victory would lead to women athletes being taken more seriously, and that was definitely accomplished."

There seemed to be no end to the stream of interesting and intriguing personalities I encountered back in those days.

One time, a group of Disneyland's "little people" joined us on a flight from Phoenix to Santa Ana, California. Some of them came on carrying their bulky costumes. That posed a problem for us because we had to find a place to stow Micky Mouse's huge head. We finally managed to shoehorn it into the DC-9's small closet, and everyone, height-challenged or not, breathed a sigh of relief. With that done, the group applied their bubbly energy to lively talk and laughter until it was time to deplane.

Around that same time, one of the tallest people in the world joined us for a flight, and this posed a whole other set of problems, because he couldn't climb the steps up to the door of the DC-9. Our ground crew had to put him on a supply truck and hoist him up and through the galley door. Then, when he finally did get into the cabin, he had to stoop over until he was able to ease himself down into the entire left front row. Once settled, his head still almost touched the cabin's ceiling and his huge hands overlapped the armrests.

I had no idea who this big guy was, but I did notice despite the difficulties he had trying to maneuver himself around, he had an utterly engaging and friendly way about him. It wasn't until just a couple of years ago, when I happened to catch *Biography* on A&E, that I found out our gentle giant was just that — André the Giant! This larger-than-life Frenchman had capitalized on his size by becoming a professional wrestler. He would even go on to have a featured role in the movie, *The Princess Bride.* Sad to say, apparently he couldn't stop his growth and his body finally gave out on him in 1993 at the age of 40.

On almost every flight back then, I encountered someone with a compelling story. One day in the summer of '96, I noticed there was an air of excitement surrounding one young woman.

When I spoke to her I said, "I'll bet you're on your way to some wonderful adventure, aren't you?" Sure enough, she told me that she was flying to Atlanta because she'd been chosen to carry the Olympic torch on its way into the stadium for the opening ceremonies.

Yes, in my thirty-seven years of flying, I've seen a whole lot of celebrities come and go. Among the ones I haven't told you about are Dick Clark, Dinah Shore, Glen Campbell, Telly Savalas, José Feliciano, George Plimpton, Lily Tomlin, Dixie Carter, B. B. King and Janet Leigh with her very young daughter, Jamie Lee Curtis. Though I wish I could, I admit I can't possibly remember them all.

But there's one more I know I'll never forget and I usually try to end my stories about famous stars with the one about him — Red Skelton. In 1983, on a flight from Reno to Las Vegas, I welcomed him and his wife into first class. "I'm so thrilled to meet you in person because I just *love* your show!" I told him. As his wife glowed with pride, Mr. Skelton beamed his big dimpled smile, thanked me and settled back for the flight.

The Skeltons were the only ones in first class, so we quickly served beverages in coach and returned to offer them extra service. It was then that I found the nerve to shyly ask one of the world's funniest men, "Mr. Skelton, we usually don't bother celebrities, but I sure would like to have your autograph."

Right away, he reached for his notepad and colored pencils and asked, "What's your name?"

"B E T T I N A," I spelled it out for him and then, to give him some time, walked away to take care of something in the galley.

When I returned after a few minutes, I was touched and delighted when he handed me a tiny, impromptu work of art. Near the top of the page he'd written *Bettina* and just below that, *Dear heart*. Then in the circle of the gigantic "R" of his autograph he had sketched a sweet clown's face.

At the time I was surprised to see how terrific his drawing was. But I've since learned that the man who had the ability to make us all laugh also had the talent to paint whimsical, poignant paintings of clowns, for which he was able to command top dollar. When I got home, I framed my priceless little treasure, and it hangs in my office today where I can glance at it for inspiration as I write this story.

In 1997, when I heard that Mr. Skelton had died, my 'dear heart' was heavy. While watching one of his older interviews that aired during the week following his death, I smiled to myself as I heard the famous redhead say, "I like being a clown and if I have touched someone in some way, I feel I have accomplished what I came here on earth to do!"

Thank you Mr. Skelton, you did indeed touch my life. And so, I think, do we all touch each other.

Yes, America has proven to be the land of many opportunities for this German immigrant girl. It's given me my flying career, a safe place to live and a country to love and grow in.

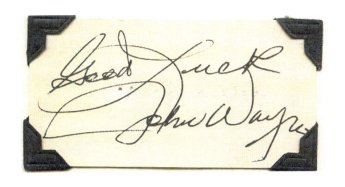

220

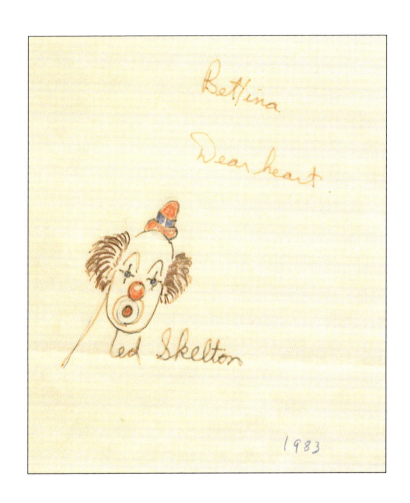

Chapter 14

The Mask and Romance

I found romance in both my public and private lives. Just before I started working for Bonanza, a former Savings & Loan client of mine, Nancy, invited me to lunch so she could introduce me to her longtime family friend, Bob Lambert. From the moment we met, we clicked. Other than his fondness for martinis, he was very much the opposite of my old flame Ray. I found him to be an intelligent man and generally very sensitive. Over the next year and a half we spent all our free time together, even after I started commuting to Scottsdale on a regular basis. I thought he was a great catch, and we knew each other well enough for what came next.

In April of '67, we were married in beautiful Arizona. On the day of the wedding, my parents arrived separately. Yes, after twenty-seven years that were mostly miserable, the two of them finally decided to go their separate ways. My mother had my little nine year old brother in tow.

Bob's parents came, too, along with his two brothers, one sister and her family. We had a small ceremony at my neighborhood Catholic church, and then we all went for a delicious, sit-down dinner at one of Scottsdale's lovely resort hotels. All in attendance said they had a good time, but all I can remember is how nervous I was for fear my parents would embarrass me with their constant sniping. I was glad when the party ended so Bob and I could retire to our honeymoon suite upstairs.

Sadly though, it soon became clear that the honeymoon was over. The two of us were certainly not a match made in heaven. Instead of happiness, all I got was a completely unmanageable lifestyle! I was commuting between Phoenix and Vegas at least four times a month, since Bonanza's headquarters had moved to Arizona. I was also taking classes twice a week at the University of Las Vegas to become a German language instructor there. I was a nervous wreck.

And I wasn't the only one overwhelmed. Bob had bought a 'fixer-upper' house before we met, and he was spending most of his spare time on that endless remodeling project. *I* couldn't understand why *he* couldn't understand the mess we were in that was so obvious to *me*. On hindsight, I've realized that our steady martini consumption made us incapable of realistically working on our relationship. We knew something had to give, but neither of us seemed to be able to come up with a solution.

Finally, after about eighteen months, I requested a separation and expressed the wish to remain friends, no matter what. Bob listened patiently, and we both agreed to that. I even suggested that we might get back together later on. I guess I was still clinging on to some hope that something would change.

Although Bob was seemingly in agreement with the reality of our situation, still he was puzzled. But, he went along with my working out the details. Two weeks later, I moved out of that dusty, unfinished house of his and into a nice place of my own in Phoenix. We stayed in touch, but it became clear to us both that we had no business getting back together. Six months later, I filed for and was granted a so-called 'friendly' divorce.

The choice to divorce made me even more miserable. I was haunted by feelings of failure as my private life collapsed. And I was consumed with guilt because I, the good Catholic girl, thought the end of my Church-sanctioned marriage would mandate automatic excommunication from

225

the religion which had forever been my home. I was sad and anxious every waking moment.

Unfortunately, however, I didn't come close to assuming responsibility for my predicament. In my dark and confused state, I went right to the top with my blame game — and pointed my finger at God. My faulty reasoning concluded that going to church and saying prayers hadn't helped me one bit. Regretfully, I turned away from God, at least for awhile. For the next twenty years, this perspective caused my inner conflicts to fester even more and drove me to lead a very turbulent life, especially in my relationships with men.

From the outside, my life may have appeared exciting, but deep down I felt totally alone and unhappy. I continued to look for love in all the wrong places — whether it was my looks, drinking or intimate, male relationships. I constantly focused on *the* Prince Charming missing from my life. All the time I wished for one to come and rescue me from my sad fate, and I looked for *him* everywhere I went. But all I kept attracting was one drunken loser after another. For some strange reason, I was especially attracted to Arizona cowboys.

The first one in that pattern was Cowboy Bob. One summer night in 1970, I went to a party at another stewardess' place in our 'singles only' apartment complex. It all began innocently enough, but around three in the morning, I began to "kibbitz" a four-man, high stakes poker game with pots bigger than any I'd ever seen. One of the players kept winking at me and flirting, seemingly unconcerned about the game at hand. That cavalier attitude, coupled with his adorable smile and sparkling blue eyes, were more than enough to attract me immediately to, you guessed it…a hard-drinking, gambling cowboy.

When the new day dawned, Bob finally quit playing and invited me join him in one for the road. The first time we

226

sat down together, I was both impressed and intrigued as he regaled me with stories about his lifestyle. He somehow convinced me that he was deeply and successfully involved in the rarefied world of Arabian show horses.

A month later—by the time I figured out he was nothing more than a hired hand, employed by rich stable owners—it was too late. All he did was transport and occasionally train or groom some of their beautiful thoroughbreds. I thought I was in love, so I went along with his delusions of grandeur. In fact, whenever I could, I even accompanied him on his assignments all around the western states as he wore a facade of wealth and prestige.

I soon discovered Bob was not the kind of man I truly needed. He had too much trouble hanging on to money and could not ever be trusted to do the right thing. Although I did not want to believe it, I also found out that he was unfaithful when I'd been flying. Not only had I confirmation that he had slept with a wealthy woman who owned a nearby ranch, but I also learned that he had some frightening connections to organized crime. This last bit of information did the trick. The very thought of being exposed to mobsters scared me just enough to want him permanently out of my life.

It took every bit of courage and negotiating skill I could muster to talk him into finally calling it quits. The whole episode left me an emotional wreck. As always, my airline family was there to comfort me or else I don't know how I would have gotten through it. But, despite my lousy track record, all too soon I found myself craving yet another relationship. It didn't take long to find another cowboy.

One crisp fall evening, my fellow stewardess friend and neighbor Donna and I decided to go out to a local bar just to get out of our houses. During the next couple of hours, we had a few drinks and danced with various partners on the small dance floor. Then, just as the two of us were about to

227

leave, we noticed a guy smiling at us from a nearby table. We thought he was so cute that we decided to stick around and motioned for him to join us, which he willingly did. When the place closed, we parted ways, but not before inviting our new friend, Jack, to a party at Donna's the following weekend.

That Saturday night, Jack showed up with his guitar and soon began serenading everyone with his sad, slow country tunes. By the time the party was over, I thought I'd found the sensitive, gifted man I'd been looking for. After our second date, I allowed myself to believe he also wanted me.

While I was off flying, he usually hung out at Kelly's, our favorite neighborhood bar. When I'd get back to town, I'd join him there and begin sipping one martini after another, wasting no time catching up to his level of drunk. I stayed with Cowboy Jack for a little over a year and went along with his fantasy of being discovered and becoming a country and western star. But the nonchalant attitude about work, constant drinking, and his infidelity became too much. In the fall of '75, I finally found the strength to break up with this disappointing man and I was once again alone.

The time outside of relationships was the most devastating for me. My tendency was to fill those days with excessive drinking and occasional one night stands. When Jack left, my pattern didn't change. I did the only thing I knew—console myself with lots of gin when I was home alone or at parties. Soon my social drinking became a big, big problem—but it was a problem I continued to deny for as long as I possibly could.

Now, as I look back to the foggy time of my life, I realize that I was spiritually depleted and always felt hopelessly and helplessly stuck. In spite of my insecurity, I kept on with flying trance-like through the turbulence of my private and public lives, all the while wearing a happy mask.

I was saved only by continued passion for my airline

life. Every time I was scheduled to fly, I proudly put on my well-fitting uniform and showed up at the airport to play the role I loved and performed extremely well. Besides the actual flights, another healthy benefit of my career that allowed me to escape misery was the free time to explore Arizona's beautiful deserts, its breathtaking mountains and lakes. In addition to free time, overnight layovers were among the perks of my job. I spent many glorious summer days in my teenage home of Edmonton, Alberta, Canada and many fiesta-filled winter evenings in beautiful Puerto Vallarta, Mexico — all courtesy of my airline employer.

I felt so much pride in both my career and my involvement in an ever growing airline industry; the number of flyers increased, many airlines merged and airports constantly expanded. The airline world progressed and so did my personal growth.

AND MY ETERNAL FLIGHT
WITH GOD CONTINUES...

You might be asking, where's the rest of the story? Originally I intended to write my memoir in one book, but in March of 2003, that changed. I realized my life story suggested three books. One aspect I have not explained in detail or emphasized was that I began therapy in the mid 1980s. I decided to share that experience and process in my second book.

During the initial composition, I found writing cathartic. I also found it exhausting and draining. Soon, it became difficult for me to fly and work on the book at the same time. Because I was re-living so much about my painful past, I knew I had to do something, so I forced myself to take a "sanity break" from writing and get back into therapy.

This time, I turned to a compassionate woman named Carol Risher who had been my therapist eight years earlier. She wasn't surprised to hear that I'd been keeping a journal right up to the point I started working on the book. Actually, I considered the book itself my ultimate journal.

I thought I had healed much of my past through my writing and spiritual practices, but I couldn't have been more wrong. With Carol's guidance, after only a few sessions, I was able to admit how much hate I still harbored...*that I didn't care at all for Self: the baby, the teenager or the woman I had been writing about.* My dear counselor reminded me that with God's Love, I first had to embrace and forgive the good, the bad, and the ugly of my past before I would ever be able to let myself honor the gift of life. Only then would I be able to write and release my books.

She also suggested that the material my editor and I had already fine-tuned should be the first book by itself. I was delighted to hear her say that, because, even though I'd thought of doing a trilogy, I'd always dismissed the idea. This time, I went along with her recommendation.

So, if you're getting enjoyment and inspiration from the book you're reading now, you have two more to look forward to--

FLYING WITH GOD--Reclaiming My Inner Spirit
and
FLYING WITH GOD--Expanding My Inner View

In Book Two, I'll share how I rescued my little girl from the darkness of her bunker, diffused my inner time bomb, and found my way back to God with both visible and invisible Help.

Book Three is about my ever-deepening relationships with God, myself, my husband, the world and how they have all affected my healing.

Since I retired from my 38-year flying career, I have a lot more time to work on the next two books--or should I say play with them--because I find that I'm enjoying writing as much as I enjoyed flying. Yes, I may be officially grounded, but I am committed to soaring ever higher.

Thank you for giving me the opportunity to serve you! I'm looking forward to traveling with you again on the next leg of our eternal journey in Book Two.

2001 AIRLINE THANKSGIVING

Attacked! Back on the horse,
With Help, set a new course.
America's 'wake-up' call,
Affects us all!

On 'auto-pilot' no more,
What is the answer to war?
What's next?" we ask in fear.
"Love's the answer!" we seem to hear.

With gratitude we go inside,
"Please help!" We find our Guide.
"See Me in your brother's eyes,
In Peace, fly even Higher Skies!"

Bettina 'Sparkles' Obernuefemann
10-25-2001

On a deeper personal note, I hope and pray that my fellow airline
employees, air travelers and everyone in our world, unite in
strength to work through their fears, especially any caused by
the events of September 11, 2001 and the on going threats and
attacks of terrorism.

FLIGHT ATTENDANT
CELEBRATES RETIREMENT

I celebrate with much gratitude! Memories come alive!
My exciting airline career began in the year of 1965.
What have I learned all these years?
Peace comes with letting go of fears!

As the sky became my home,
I knew I was never alone.
Soaring above conflicts with and expanded view,
I learned to be kinder to me and you.

As one door closes, I keep love for flying in my heart.
Another door opens; I have freedom to play a new part.
Beginning another leg of life's journey in harmony,
I continue to serve and fly with God, eternally.

Bettina 'Sparkles' Obernuefemann
July, 2003

To Order Books or Contact:
Bettina "Sparkles" Obernuefemann

Call Toll Free:
(877) 202-1940

Em: sparkles@BettinaSparkles.com

Mail:
Box 254
Norfork, AR 72658

Send $25 USD
with Name & Shipping Address

BIOGRAPHY

Bettina "Sparkles" Obernuefemann was born in Germany and presently lives in north central Arkansas, with her husband Michael. July 31, 2003 she retired after a thirty-eight year flying career. She's devoting her new 'free' time to writing, a creative effort blending her love for flying with her dedication to recovery and spirituality. Sparkles and Michael have another dream — to develop a wildlife animal sanctuary and a vacation retreat on their 130-acre property 'Harmony Hills'—located in the beautiful Ozark Mountains.

Sparkles early in her flying career, 1966.   *Sparkles at time of retirement, 2003.*